Healing Your Emotional Self

Healing Your Emotional Self

A Powerful Program to Help You Raise Your Self-Esteem, Quiet Your Inner Critic, and Overcome Your Shame

BEVERLY ENGEL

John Wiley & Sons, Inc.

Published by John Wiley & Sons, Inc., Hoboken, New Jersey
Published simultaneously in Canada

For general information about our other products and services, please contact our Customer Care Department within the United States at (800) 762-2974, outside the United States at (317) 572-3993 or fax (317) 572-4002.

Wiley also publishes its books in a variety of electronic formats. Some content that appears in print may not be available in electronic books. For more information about Wiley products, visit our web site at www.wiley.com.

Library of Congress Cataloging-in-Publication Data:
Engel, Beverly.
    Healing your emotional self : a powerful program to help you raise your self-esteem, quiet your inner critic, and overcome your shame / Beverly Engel.
        p. cm.
    Includes bibliographical references and index.
    ISBN-13 978-0-471-72567-1 (cloth)
    ISBN-10 0-471-72567-6 (cloth)
    1. Mental health. 2. Self-esteem. 3. Self-care, Health. 4. Psychology, Pathological. I. Title.
    RA790.E555 2006
    158.1—dc22

Printed in the United States of America

10 9 8 7 6 5 4 3 2 1

This book is dedicated to the memory of those who lost their lives in the tsunami in December 2004 and to all the people who worried about me while I was in India. The experience taught me a valuable lesson and reminded me of how many people love me—a lesson those of us who were abused continually need to relearn.

Contents

PART FOUR
Specialized Help

Acknowledgments

I feel so fortunate and so grateful to work once again with Tom Miller, my wonderful editor at John Wiley & Sons. I appreciate his wise feedback and am grateful for the fact that he has gone to bat for me over and over. His faith in me has been unremitting, and it has helped me to continue to have faith in myself. I wish to thank everyone at Wiley who worked on this book, especially Lisa Burstiner, who did an economical yet astute job of editing.

To my fabulous agent, Stedman Mays, I offer my undying gratitude and appreciation. You have gone way, way beyond the call of duty for me. I appreciate all your hard work, your feedback, your suggestions, your intuition, and most of all your dedication.

I also want to express my gratitude for Mary Tahan, my other agent. Mary, I appreciate your insights and suggestions regarding my books, and I especially appreciate all your hard work when it comes to selling my foreign rights. I always know you are pulling for me.

I am deeply appreciative of the numerous clients who were willing to try my Mirror Therapy techniques. Your courage, determination, and feedback are greatly appreciated.

I am deeply indebted to the work of two authors whose work I called upon for this book: Elan Golumb, Ph.D., author of *Trapped in the Mirror: Adult Children of Narcissists in Their Struggle for Self*; and Byron Brown, author of *Soul without Shame: A Guide to Liberating Yourself from the Judge Within*. Their wonderful work illuminated and inspired me.

I am also indebted to the work of two people whose ideas inspired me to create my Mirror Therapy program. Arthur P. Ciaramicoli, Ed.D., Ph.D., the author of *The Power of Empathy: A Practical Guide to Creating Intimacy, Self-Understanding and Lasting Love*, provided me a framework from which to work, especially with regard to having empathy for oneself. Laurel Mellin, creator of the Solutions Program and author of *The Pathway*, has helped me to further understand the damage caused by inadequate parenting. And while I already understood the importance of creating a nurturing inner voice (symbolic of a healthy mother), Laurel taught me that it is equally important to create healthy limits (symbolic of a strong father).

Introduction

THERE ARE THOUSANDS OF PEOPLE who were emotionally abused, neglected, or smothered by their parents or other significant caretakers when they were growing up. Many of these people do not realize they were abused or neglected, and they continue to suffer from myriad problems throughout their lives because they are not getting the help they need. People who internalize the abuse manifest self-destructiveness, depression, suicidal thoughts, passivity, withdrawal (avoidance of social contacts), shyness, and a low degree of communication with others. They are likely to have low self-esteem and may suffer from feelings of guilt and remorse, depression, loneliness, rejection, and resignation. Perceiving themselves as unworthy and the world as a hostile place in which they are bound to fail, many are unwilling to try new tasks, develop new skills, or take risks.

People who externalize the abuse may be unpredictable and violent, their behavior characterized by impulsive action rather than conformity to social norms. They frequently become anxious, aggressive, and hostile. They suffer from constant fear and are always on the alert and ready to hit back. Many end up mistreating others, often in the same ways they were mistreated.

At the core of all these symptoms and behaviors is an inadequately developed sense of self and a distorted image of self based on parental negative messages and treatment. Unless adult survivors address these fundamental issues, their efforts toward recovery will be thwarted.

If you were a victim of emotional abuse or neglect as a child, this book will show you exactly what you need to do in order to heal from the damage done to your self-image and self-esteem. *Healing Your Emotional Self* will guide you step by step through a program that is both innovative and psychologically sound—innovative because it uses the mirror as a metaphor and a tool for healing, and psychologically sound because it combines my many years of experience specializing in treating people who have been emotionally abused with various respected psychological concepts.

Although the primary audience for this book is survivors of emotional abuse and neglect, this book is for anyone who suffers from low self-esteem or body-image issues. People who are preoccupied with their bodies, or who determine their self-worth by how their bodies look, will find the book particularly helpful. Many suffer from a distorted body image and from negative feelings concerning their bodies, but they do not understand that the cause may be negative parental messages, emotional abuse, or neglect.

Many of you know me from my other books on emotional abuse, namely: *The Emotionally Abusive Relationship*, *The Emotionally Abused Woman*, and *Encouragements for the Emotionally Abused Woman*. In those books I wrote about the fact that people who are currently being emotionally abused (or are abusive) are doing so because they were emotionally abused as children. Now, in *Healing Your Emotional Self*, I will help readers take a giant step forward by offering a powerful program that will help them repair the damage caused by emotionally abusive parents.

Childhood neglect and emotional abuse cause many of the most serious problems people suffer from today. This is not a revelation to most professionals or to many who suffer from its effects, but in spite of this knowledge, there is insufficient help for the survivors of these types of abuse. Relatively few books have offered readers a complete understanding of how this kind of child abuse affects people, ways to heal from the damage, and how to resolve relationships with parents. This is the first book to offer a comprehensive healing program specific to the kinds of messages (mirrors) that emotionally abusive and neglectful parents give their children and to how this kind of abuse affects a child's self-image.

Neglect and emotional abuse are the primary causes of both borderline personality disorder (BPD) and narcissistic personality disorder (NPD), which have turned out to be *the* disorders of our time. This is true for two major reasons: Children in the past two decades have grown up with absent, neglectful parents and parents who continued to pass on the emotional abuse they themselves sustained. In addition, both the borderline and narcissistic personality disorders have "come out of the closet" in terms of professionals telling their patients exactly what their diagnoses are. In the past they had kept these diagnoses from their clients for fear of traumatizing them.

Those who were emotionally abused or neglected also tend to suffer from eating disorders. Many overeat as a way of soothing themselves, while others overeat out of self-loathing. On the other end of the spectrum, many become anorexic as a way of gaining a sense of control because they feel overly controlled by their parents.

People recovering from alcohol or drug abuse will also find this book helpful because many addicts suffer from severe distortions to their sense of self.

In *Healing Your Emotional Self* I offer my unique Mirror Therapy program for healing, which has proven to be highly effective with my clients and the clients of some of my colleagues. This program is highly innovative, combining what I have learned from many years of specializing with adults who were emotionally abused or neglected as children with concepts from developmental psychology, object relations, self psychology, body therapies, cognitive behavioral therapy, and art therapy. Many of the ideas in the book are uniquely my own, while others are variations on the concepts created by other people, and together they form a unique program designed specifically for the emotionally abused or neglected.

For example, according Laurel Mellin M.A., R.D., author of *The Pathway* and creator of the Solutions Program, research on childhood obesity from San Francisco University shows that for the children studied, most of their extra weight was rooted in the most basic internal patterns of their functioning—the inner conversations they had with themselves. Teaching the kids some very basic skills— self-nurturing (which is like having a responsive internal mother) and setting effective limits (which is like having a safe, powerful father within)—brought their minds and bodies into balance and allowed their drive to overeat to fade. These skills can be taught to people of any age and are effective for other common excesses such as drinking, smoking, overspending, and working. The skills find their way into the thinking brain—our emotional core. I have adapted some of these skills to help adults who were emotionally abused or deprived to essentially "grow themselves up" and give themselves the skills their parents did not give them.

This book will not simply cover old ground. While I will spend some time defining emotional abuse and describing its effects, I focus primarily on healing, especially in regard to helping readers to raise their self-esteem and improve their self-image. (Refer to my earlier books *The Emotionally Abused Woman*, *Encouragements for the Emotionally Abused Woman*, and *The Emotionally Abusive Relationship* for more information on emotional abuse and its effects.)

I have organized this book around several themes, including "The Seven Types of Emotionally Abusive or Neglectful Parents" and "The Seven Most Common Parental Mirrors." I provide specific advice and strategies for healing for each of the destructive parental mirrors and specific strategies for dealing with each of the seven types of emotionally abusive parents—all using my Mirror Therapy concepts and strategies.

There are other unique aspects to *Healing Your Emotional Self*. Most of my books on emotional abuse have been focused on the issue of *relationships*—how adults who were abused or neglected as children can avoid losing themselves in their relationships, how they can avoid being reabused, and how they can avoid passing on the abuse to a partner or to their children. *Healing Your Emotional Self* focuses on the *self*—how readers can become reunited with the self, how they can create a positive self separate from their abusive parents' distorted picture of them, and how they can raise their self-esteem. In addition, the book focuses on helping readers to overcome their tendency toward self-blame, self-hatred, and self-destructiveness.

I also cover a subject that has not been focused on in self-help books: the effects on adults who experienced parental neglect in childhood. Many who were neglected will continually search for someone who will give to them what they missed out on in their childhood. This naturally sets them up to be used, victimized, or abused by their partners. Others suffer from a constant feeling of worthlessness, emptiness, deep loneliness, and confusion, and they are unable to sustain intimate relationships.

I will also discuss another issue that is seldom if ever covered in most self-help books—the effects of parental smothering on a child—which can be just as damaging as neglect.

Many people are preoccupied with their looks and even more are critical of them. While some depend on diets, exercise regimes, and cosmetic surgery to help them like what they see in the mirror, others recognize that they will never be happy with what they see unless they raise their self-esteem. This book takes raising your self-esteem to an entirely different level. It teaches a system that can actually help heal the damage caused by negative parental messages.

PART ONE

How Your Parents Shaped Your Self-Esteem, Self-Image, and Body Image

1

Our Parents as Mirrors

Perfectionism is self-abuse of the highest order.

—Ann Wilson Schaef

I avoid looking in the mirror as much as I possibly can. When I do look, all I see are my imperfections—my long nose, my crooked teeth, my small breasts. Other people tell me I'm attractive, but I just don't see it.

—Kristin, age twenty-six

I'm what you would call a perfectionist, especially when it comes to my work. It takes me twice as long as it does other people to get something done, because I have to go over it a dozen times to make sure I haven't made any mistakes. My boss complains about my being so slow, but I'd rather have him complain about that than have him find a mistake. That would devastate me.

—Elliot, age thirty-one

There's a voice inside my head that constantly chastises me with "Why did you do that?" "Why did you say that?" The criticism is relentless. Nothing I ever do is right. I'm never good enough. Sometimes I just feel like screaming—Shut up! Leave me alone!

—Teresa, age forty-three

I don't know what it will take for me to finally feel good about myself. I keep thinking I need to do more, achieve more, be a better person, and then I'll like myself. Other people are impressed with how much I've achieved in my life, but it doesn't seem to matter how much I do; I'm never good enough for me.
                                        —Charles, age fifty-five

DO YOU RELATE TO ANY of these people? Do you have a difficult time looking in the mirror because you never like what you see? Do you find that you are never pleased with yourself, no matter how much effort you put into making yourself a better person, no matter how much work you do on your body? Do you constantly find fault in yourself? Are you a perfectionist? Are you plagued by an inner critic who constantly berates you or finds something wrong with everything you do? Or are you like Charles, who believes that the way to feeling good about yourself is through your accomplishments—yet no matter how much you accomplish it is never enough?

Many of us focus a great deal of time and attention on improving our bodies and making ourselves more attractive. Yet, for all the time and money spent on dieting, exercise, clothes, and cosmetic surgery, many still do not like who they see in the mirror. There is always something that needs to be changed or improved.

People who are critical of how they look are usually critical of other aspects of themselves as well. They tend to focus on their flaws rather than their assets, and they are seldom pleased with their performance—whether at work, at school, or in a relationship. They chastise themselves mercilessly when they make a mistake.

There is nothing wrong with wanting to improve yourself; everyone suffers from time to time with self-critical thoughts. But some people have such low self-esteem that they are never satisfied with their achievements, their physical appearance, or their performance. They have a relentless inner critic who constantly tears them down and robs them of any satisfaction they might temporarily feel when they have reached a goal. The following questionnaire will help you determine whether you are suffering from low self-esteem and an unhealthy inner critic.

Questionnaire: A "Self" Examination

1. Do you suffer from insecurity or a lack of confidence?
2. Do you focus more on what you do wrong or what you fail at than what you do right or well?
3. Do you feel less than or not as good as other people because you are not perfect in what you do or how you look?
4. Do you believe you need to do more, be more, or give more in order to earn the respect and love of other people?
5. Are you aware of having a critical inner voice that frequently tells you that you did something wrong?
6. Are you constantly critical of your performance—at work, at school, at sports?
7. Are you critical of the way you interact with others? For example, do you frequently kick yourself for saying the wrong thing or for behaving in certain ways around others?
8. Do you feel like a failure—in life, in your career, in your relationships?
9. Are you a perfectionist?
10. Do you feel like you do not deserve good things? Do you become anxious when you are successful or happy?
11. Are you afraid that if people knew the real you, they wouldn't like you? Are you afraid people will find out you are a fraud?
12. Are you frequently overwhelmed with shame and embarrassment because you feel exposed, made fun of, or ridiculed?
13. Do you constantly compare yourself to others and come up short?
14. Do you avoid looking in the mirror as much as possible, or do you tend to look in the mirror a lot to make sure you look okay?

15. Are you usually critical of what you see when you look in the mirror? Are you seldom, if ever, satisfied with the way you look?

16. Are you self-conscious or embarrassed about the way you look?

17. Do you have an eating disorder—compulsive overeating, bingeing and purging, frequent dieting or starvation, or anorexia?

18. Do you need to drink alcohol or take other substances in order to feel comfortable or less self-conscious in social situations?

19. Do you fail to take very good care of yourself through poor diet, not enough sleep, or too little or too much exercise?

20. Do you tend to be self-destructive by smoking, abusing alcohol or drugs, or speeding?

21. Have you ever deliberately hurt yourself, that is, cut yourself?

If you answered yes to more than five of these questions, you need the special help this book provides in order to raise your self-esteem, quiet your inner critic, heal your shame, and begin to find real joy and satisfaction in your achievements and accomplishments.

Even if you only answered yes to one of these questions, this book can help you because it isn't natural or healthy to experience any of those feelings. You were born with an inherent sense of goodness, strength, and wisdom that you should be able to call upon in moments of self-doubt. Unfortunately, you may have lost touch with this inner sense because of the way you were raised and by the messages you received to the contrary.

Self-Esteem Defined

Let's start by defining self-esteem and differentiating it from *self-image* and *self-concept*. *Self-esteem* is how you feel about yourself as a person—your overall judgment of yourself. Your self-esteem may be high or low, depending on how much you like or approve of yourself. If you have high self-esteem, you have an appreciation of the full extent of your personality. This means that you accept yourself for who you are, with both your good qualities and your so-called bad ones. It can be assumed that you have self-respect, self-love, and feelings of self-worth. You don't need to impress others because you already know you have value. If you are unsure whether you have high self-esteem, ask yourself: "Do I believe that I am lovable?" "Do I believe I am worthwhile?"

Our feelings of self-worth form the core of our personality. Nothing is as important to our psychological well-being. The level of our self-esteem affects virtually every aspect of our lives. It affects how we perceive ourselves and how others perceive us, and how they subsequently treat us. It affects our choices in life, from our careers to whom we befriend or get involved with romantically. It influences how we get along with others and how productive we are, as well as how much use we make of our aptitudes and abilities. It affects our ability to take action when things need to be changed and our ability to be creative. It affects our stability, and it even affects whether we tend to be followers or leaders. It only stands to reason that the level of our self-esteem, the way we feel about ourselves in general, would also affect our ability to form intimate relationships.

Many people use the words *self-esteem* and *self-concept* interchangeably, but these terms actually have different meanings. Our self-concept, or self-image, is the set of beliefs or images we have about ourselves. Our self-esteem is the measure of how much we like and approve of our self-concept. Another way of thinking about it is that self-esteem is how much respect you have for yourself, while self-image is how you see yourself. Still another way of differentiating between self-esteem and self-image is to think of self-esteem as something you give to yourself (that's why it is called self-esteem) and self-image is usually based on how you imagine others perceive you.

Our self-image is made up of a wide variety of images and beliefs. Some of these are self-evident and easily verifiable (for example, "I am a woman," "I am a therapist"). But there are also other, less tangible aspects of the self (for example, "I am intelligent," "I am competent").

Many of the ideas we have about ourselves were acquired in childhood from two sources: how others treated us and what others told us about ourselves. How others defined us has thus become how we now perceive ourselves. Your *self-image*—who you think you are—is a package that you have put together from how others have seen and treated you, and from the conclusions you drew in comparing yourself to others.

The Real Cause of Your Low Self-Esteem or Negative Self-Image

The primary cause of your low self-esteem or negative self-image probably goes back to your childhood. No matter what has happened to you in your life, your parents (or the people who raised you) have the most significant influence on how you feel about yourself. Negative parental behavior and messages can have a profound effect on our self-image and self-esteem. This is especially true of survivors of emotional abuse, neglect, or smothering as a child.

Inadequate, unhealthy parenting can affect the formation of a child's identity, self-concept, and level of self-esteem. Research clearly shows that the single most important factor in determining the amount of self-esteem a child starts out with is his or her parents' style of child-rearing during the first three or four years of the child's life.

When parents are loving, encouraging, and fair-minded, and provide proper discipline and set appropriate limits, the children they shape end up being self-confident, self-monitoring, and self-actualized. But when parents are neglectful, critical, and unfair, and provide harsh discipline and inappropriate limits, the children they shape are insecure and self-critical, and they suffer from low self-esteem.

When I first met Matthew I was struck by his dark good looks. He resembled a younger, taller, more exotic-looking Tom Cruise, with his chiseled features, his large, dark, almond-shaped eyes, and his straight dark hair. Because he was so strikingly good-looking I expected him to speak to me with confidence, but instead he spoke in a reticent, almost apologetic way. As he explained to me why he had come to therapy, I discovered that he felt extremely insecure. Although he was an intelligent, talented, attractive young man, he was tormented with self-doubt and was extremely critical of himself. Why would a young man with so much going for him feel so badly about himself?

As Matthew told me the story of his life, I discovered his father was never pleased with him. No matter what Matthew did, it was never enough. He told me about a time when he got on the honor roll in school and was excited to tell his father about it. Instead of congratulating Matthew and being proud of him, his father told him that since school was so easy for him he needed to get a job after school. So Matthew did as his father suggested. But this didn't seem to please him, either. Instead, his father complained that he wasn't helping out enough with yard work and that he needed to quit his job. "You're just working so you can make money to waste on girls," his father criticized, somehow not remembering that he had been the one to pressure Matthew into getting a job in the first place. Matthew had an interest in music and was a very talented piano player. But his father wasn't happy about his taking lessons. "You're already too effeminate," he scoffed. "Why don't you go out for sports like I did in school?" When Matthew followed his father's advice and tried out for the track team, his father complained, "It just doesn't have the same prestige as playing football or basketball. Why don't you try out for one of those teams?"

Because his father was never proud of him and never acknowledged his accomplishments, Matthew became very hard on himself. He became very self-critical; no matter what he accomplished he found something wrong with it. If someone did try to compliment him, he pushed their praise away with statements such as "Oh, anyone could have done that," or "Yeah, but you should have seen how I messed up yesterday."

By not acknowledging Matthew and by never being pleased, Matthew's father had caused him to be self-conscious and fearful. Many parents undermine their children's self-esteem and create in them a sort of "self anxiety" by treating them in any or all of the following ways: with a lack of warmth and affection, acknowledgment, respect, or admiration, as well as with unreasonable expectations, domination, indifference, belittling, isolation, or unfair or unequal treatment.

"Inner Critic" Defined

Having a strong inner critic is another factor in creating low self-esteem, and it usually goes hand in hand with low self-esteem. Your inner critic is formed through the normal socialization process that every child experiences. Parents teach their children which behaviors are acceptable and which are unacceptable, dangerous, or morally wrong. Most parents do this by praising the former and discouraging the latter. Children know (either consciously or unconsciously) that their parents are the source of all physical and emotional nourishment, so parental approval feels like a matter of life or death to them. Therefore, when they are scolded or spanked they feel the withdrawal of parental approval very acutely because it carries with it the horrible risk of losing all support.

All children retain conscious and unconscious memories of those times when they felt wrong or bad because of the loss of their parents' approval. This is where the inner critic gets his start. (I use "he" when referring to the inner critic because many people, including women, think of their inner critic as being male. Feel free to substitute "she" if it feels more appropriate for you.) Even as an adult there is still a part of you that believes you are "bad" whenever someone gets angry with you or when you make a mistake.

Your inner critic's voice is the voice of a disapproving parent—the punishing, forbidding voice that shaped your behavior as a child. If your early experiences were mild and appropriate, your adult critic may only rarely attack, but if you were given very strong messages about your "badness" or "wrongness" as a child, your adult critic will attack you frequently and fiercely.

Emotional Abuse and Neglect Defined

Abuse is a very emotionally powerful word. It usually implies intent or even malice on the part of the abuser. But parents who emotionally abuse or neglect their children seldom do so intentionally. Most are simply repeating the way they were treated as a child—doing to their children what was done to them. Many do not realize that the way they are treating their children is harmful to them; few do so out of malice—an intentional desire to hurt their children.

Low self-esteem is not usually instilled in children through conscious or deliberate efforts on the part of the parents. Typically, parents of children with low self-esteem had low self-esteem themselves. And those parents who emotionally abuse, neglect, or smother their children usually do not recognize the tremendous power they have in shaping their children's sense of self.

We need to be very specific when we use the words *emotional abuse*. Emotional abuse of a child is a pattern of behavior—meaning that it occurs on a continuous basis, over time. Occasional negative attitudes or actions are not considered emotional abuse. Even the best of parents have occasions when they have momentarily lost control and said hurtful things to their children, failed to give them the attention they wanted, or unintentionally scared them by their actions. Every parent undoubtedly treats their children in some of these ways from time to time, but emotionally abusive parents regularly treat their children in some or all of these ways.

Emotional abuse of a child is a pattern of behavior that attacks a child's emotional development and sense of self-worth. Because emotional abuse affects a child's sense of self, the victim comes to view himself or herself as unworthy of love and affection. Emotional abuse includes both acts and omissions by parents or caretakers, and it can cause serious behavioral, cognitive, emotional, or mental disorders in a child. This form of maltreatment includes:

- Verbal abuse (including constant criticism, ridiculing, blaming, belittling, insulting, rejecting, and inappropriate teasing)

- Placing excessive or unreasonable demands on a child that are beyond his or her capabilities

- Being overly controlling

- Emotionally smothering a child (including being overprotective or unwilling to allow the child to create a separate life from her parents)

- Rejecting or emotionally abandoning a child (including being cold and unresponsive and withholding love)

Neglect is an even more misunderstood word and can manifest itself physically and emotionally. *Physical neglect* includes failure on the part of a parent or primary caregiver to provide for the child's basic physical needs (food, water, shelter, attention to hygiene) as well as his or her emotional, social, environmental, and medical needs. It also includes failure to provide adequate supervision.

Emotional neglect includes failure to provide the nurturing and positive support necessary for a child's emotional and psychological growth and development—providing little or no love, support, or guidance. This includes inattention to a child's needs for acknowledgment, affection, and emotional support (being uninterested in a child's feelings, activities, and problems).

The following questionnaire will further help you to understand emotional abuse and neglect and to determine whether you experienced them as a child.

QUESTIONNAIRE: WERE YOU EMOTIONALLY ABUSED, NEGLECTED, OR SMOTHERED AS A CHILD?

1. Was one or both of your parents overly critical of you? Were you frequently criticized for saying the wrong things or behaving in the wrong way? Did one or both of your parents often criticize the way you looked?

2. Was it impossible to please your parents? Did you get the impression that no matter what you did, your parents would never approve of you?

3. Were your parents perfectionists? Were you chastised or punished unless you did things in a certain way?

4. Did your parents tell you that you were bad, worthless, or stupid, or that you would never amount to anything? Did they call you insulting names?

5. Did your parents belittle you, make fun of you, or make you the object of malicious or sadistic jokes?

6. Did your parents ignore your physical needs, for example, failing to provide adequate clothing such as a warm coat in the winter, or not providing adequate medical care?

7. Did your parents force you to live in dangerous or unstable environments (such as exposure to domestic violence or parental conflict)?

8. Were your parents so preoccupied or busy with their own needs or problems that they didn't take time to be with you?

9. Did your parents frequently leave you alone to fend for yourself? Were you deprived of physical nurturing (for example, being held or comforted when you were upset) or affection when you were a child?

10. Was one of both of your parents distant or aloof toward you as a child?

11. Did one or both of your parents have a drinking problem or an addiction to drugs or gambling, or any other addiction that caused one or both to neglect you?

12. Were you ever abandoned as a child (were you ever sent away to live with someone else as a punishment or because a parent was sick or could not take care of you)?

13. Was one or both of your parents overly protective of you or overly fearful that harm would come to you (for example, not allowing you to participate in sports or normal childhood activities for fear of your getting hurt)?

14. Did one or both of your parents isolate you from others or refuse to allow you to have friends over or to go over to other children's homes?

15. Was one or both of your parents overly possessive of you (that is, did he or she appear jealous if you paid attention to anyone else or if you had a friend or romantic partner)?

16. Did one or both parents treat you as a confidante or seek emotional comfort from you? Did you often feel as if you were the parent and your parents were the children?

These questions describe various forms of emotional abuse and neglect. If you answered yes to any of questions 1 through 5, you were emotionally abused through verbal abuse or unreasonable expectations. If you answered yes to any of questions 6 through 12, you were neglected or abandoned as a child. If you answered yes to any of questions 13 through 16, you suffered from emotional smothering or emotional incest.

Psychological Maltreatment

Although most emotional abuse and neglect is unintentional on a parent's part, sometimes parents deliberately inflict harm on their children in these ways. *Psychological maltreatment* is a term used by professionals to describe a concerted attack by an adult on a child's development of self and social competence—a pattern of psychically destructive behavior. Sometimes coming under the category of emotional abuse, there are five major behavioral forms:

- Rejecting—behaviors that communicate or constitute abandonment of the child, such as a refusal to show affection
- Isolating—preventing the child from participating in normal opportunities for social interaction
- Terrorizing—threatening the child with severe or sinister punishment, or deliberately developing a climate of fear or threat
- Ignoring—where the caregiver is psychologically unavailable to the child and fails to respond to the child's behavior
- Corrupting—caregiver behavior that encourages the child to develop false social values that reinforce antisocial or deviant behavioral patterns such as aggression, criminal acts, or substance abuse

How Children Are Affected by Emotional Abuse and Neglect

The primary way that children are affected by emotional abuse and neglect is that their self-image becomes distorted, they lack a strong sense of self, they develop extremely low self-esteem, and their emotional development is thwarted. Emotional abuse and neglect create a distorted view of oneself as unacceptable, unlovable, or "less than" others. Emotional abuse, neglect, and smothering can also create self-hatred in a child. Many children who are emotionally abused or neglected exhibit extremes in either passivity or aggressiveness. Children who are constantly shamed, humiliated, terrorized, or rejected suffer at least as much as, if not more than, if they had been physically assaulted. Studies have found that neglect can be more damaging than outright abuse. A survey of maltreated children found that neglected children were the most anxious, inattentive, and apathetic, and that they often tended to be alternatively aggressive and withdrawn.

There are various reasons for this outcome. Neglect and abandonment communicate to a child that he or she is not worthy of love and care. Early emotional deprivation often produces babies who grow into anxious and insecure children who are slow to develop or who have low self-esteem. This is particularly true of babies who were given inadequate amounts of physical touch and holding. Researchers have found that the healthiest children are those who were frequently held and caressed by their parents. Children who were deprived of touch became what is called "touch avoidant." By the age of six, these children would refuse nurturing touch.

Emotional abuse often includes communicating to a child, either verbally or nonverbally, that he or she is unlovable, ugly, stupid, or wicked. Both neglect and emotional abuse can cause children to search within themselves for the faults that merit their parents' bad treatment. Such internalized rejection can take a heavy toll on a child's developing self, leading to poor self-image and low self-esteem. Children who are shown little empathy and given little praise and acceptance often exhibit not only poor self-esteem but also self-destructive behavior, apathy, and depression. Children who experience a chaotic environment with little security and safety tend to exhibit anxiety, fear, and night terrors. If they are threatened with the withdrawal of love from their parents or primary caretakers, they often experience severe anxiety, excessive fear, and dependency.

A literature review of the effects of emotional abuse on children conducted by Marti Tamm Loring, author of *Emotional Abuse*, revealed the following:

Those who internalize the abuse become depressed, suicidal, and withdrawn. They manifest self-destructiveness, depression, suicidal thoughts, passivity, withdrawal (avoidance of social contacts), shyness, and a low degree of communication with others. They are likely to have low self-esteem and may suffer from feelings of guilt and remorse, depression, loneliness, rejection, and resignation. Perceiving themselves as unworthy and the world as a hostile place in which they are bound to fail, many are unwilling to try new tasks or develop new skills.

People who externalize the abuse frequently become anxious, aggressive, and hostile, may suffer from constant fear, and are always ready to "hit back." As Louise M. Wisechild, the author of *The Mother I Carry*, a wonderful memoir about healing from emotional abuse, so eloquently wrote:

> Emotional abuse is like water dripping every day on a stone, leaving a depression, eroding the personality by an unrelenting accumulation of incidents that humiliate or ridicule or dismiss. Emotional abuse is air and piercing vibration. Emotional abuse can feel physical even though no hand has been raised. The perpetrator may seem fragile and pathetic but still be vicious. Childhood emotional abuse can define us when we are young, debilitate us as we grow older, and spread like a virus as we take its phrases and turn them on others.

Note that emotional abuse is typically associated with and a result of other types of abuse and neglect. Emotional abuse is the core of all forms of abuse, and the long-term effects of child abuse and neglect generally stem from the emotional aspects of abuse.

The Role of Shame in Creating Low Self-Esteem and Perfectionism

Shame is a feeling deep within us of being exposed and unworthy. When we feel shamed we want to hide. We hang our heads, stoop our shoulders, and curve inward as if trying to make ourselves invisible.

Emotional abuse and neglect are very shaming experiences, and those who are victimized in any way feel humiliated and degraded by the experience. In addition, most children blame themselves for the way their parents treated them, feeling that somehow they deserved to be treated in such a way and thinking, "If I'd only minded my mother, she wouldn't have belittled and yelled at me in front of my friends." This is an attempt to regain some sense of power and control. To blame oneself and assume one could have done better or could have prevented an incident is more tolerable than to face the reality of utter helplessness.

Children raised by parents who frequently scolded, criticized, or spanked them whenever they did the slightest thing wrong end up feeling that their very being is wrong—not just their actions. Some people fight against shame by striving for perfection. This is a way of compensating for an underlying sense of defectiveness. The reasoning (although subconscious) goes like this: "If I can become perfect, I'll never be shamed again." This quest for perfection is, of course, doomed to fail. Since the person suffering shame already feels inherently not good enough, nothing he or she does will ever be perceived as good enough. Therefore, continuing to expect perfection in yourself will cause you to constantly be disappointed and constantly damage your self-esteem.

How Emotional Abuse and Neglect Affect Your Sense of Self

I've used lots of words so far to identify different aspects of the self, such as self-image, self-concept, and self-esteem, but as yet I haven't defined the concept of *self*. There are many definitions, but for our purposes we'll define it as *your inner core*. It is the sense you have of yourself as a separate person—the sense of where your needs and feelings leave off and others' begin.

There is another "self" phrase that needs defining: *sense of self*. This is your internal awareness of who you are and how you fit into the world. The ideal is what is referred to as "a coherent sense of self," which is having an internal feeling of solidarity. You experience yourself as a person who has a place in the world, who has a right to express yourself, and who has the power to affect and participate in what happens to you. Unfortunately, people who were emotionally abused or neglected in childhood possess a sense of self that is often characterized by feelings that are anything but empowering. Instead, they feel helpless, ashamed, enraged, terrified, and guilty, leading to feelings of insecurity.

We are not necessarily in touch with our sense of self until something happens to make us pay attention to it. If someone dismisses your accomplishments or rejects you, your focus will turn inward. You will begin to question whether you are worthy or loveable. The reverse can also be true. If someone compliments you, you might turn inward to congratulate yourself. Being self-conscious means that for whatever reason, you have become preoccupied with how you are doing or how you are coming across to other people. This self-evaluation can become obsessive and can cause you either to feel inhibited in the company of others or to put on a show for them. Either way, self-consciousness interferes with your ability to be your authentic self.

When we feel ignored or rejected by others (especially our parents), we often begin to worry about what we might have done to warrant this reaction. This begins early in life. Children are egocentric—meaning they assume everything centers around them and therefore they must be the cause of others' reactions—and so they tend to blame themselves for the way others treat them. As we grow older we become self-conscious and we feed our self-consciousness with a lot of self-deprecating assumptions.

In order to develop a strong sense of self you needed to be raised in an environment where positive psychological nourishment was available. Positive psychological nourishment consists of the following:

- *Empathetic responses.* When we say that someone has the ability to empathize, we generally mean she has the space inside to listen and respond to another person without getting caught up, or stuck, in her own point of view. She has the ability to put herself in the other person's place—to imagine how the other person feels. Unfortunately, many parents are so caught up in themselves that they have no room for anyone else's needs or views—even their own children's. A typical nonempathetic response from a parent may take the form of getting impatient with a baby who soils his pants when the parent is busy trying to get ready for a party. An empathetic parent will take a deep breath, pick up her toddler lovingly, and remind herself that the baby can't help it. She'll talk sweetly to the child and caress him gently as she changes his diaper. A nonempathetic parent may blame the child for causing a delay, handle the child roughly, and communicate displeasure toward him.

• *Having your perceptions validated.* One of the primary ways of encouraging a healthy sense of self is for parents to validate a child's experience, such as when a parent agrees that something is sad when the child feels sad. This kind of validation usually causes the child to experience a feeling of being all right. She feels that she is "on target" with her feelings and probably also feels less alone in the world. If, on the other hand, a parent tells the child that a sad thing is really a happy thing, the child might suddenly feel off balance or that something is wrong with her. She will also probably feel very alone.

• *Having your uniqueness respected.* When a child's uniqueness as an individual is respected, he learns to tolerate differences in himself and others. He learns that it is interesting to discover differences and to deal with them constructively. Unfortunately, in many families it isn't considered normal for people in the same family to have different preferences. Instead, there is an assumption that when a child has a different preference or disagrees, he is trying to control his caretakers or is involved in a power struggle. Some are even punished or blamed for being different from other family members. This is translated, in the child's mind, to the message "I am bad." When a child's individual preferences are respected, on the other hand, he tends to feel, "I am all right." This in turn promotes a sense of self characterized by feeling worthwhile and loved.

How Parents Act as Mirrors

Infants have no "sense of self," that is, no internal knowledge of who they are as a person separate from everyone else. If an infant were to look in the mirror, she would not recognize herself. You've no doubt watched the reaction of infants or toddlers who look in a mirror. They often react as if they were seeing another child.

Parents act as a mirror to show a child who he is. If a baby's parents smile at him, he learns that he is delightful and adorable. If a baby is held and comforted, he learns that he is safe. If his parents respond to his crying, he learns that he is important and effective. But if a baby is not held, spoken to, comforted, rocked, and loved, he learns other lessons about his worth. If his cries are not responded to, he learns helplessness; he learns he is not important. Later, as the child grows, his parents will act as a mirror in other ways. If they overprotect him, he will learn he is incompetent. If they are overly controlling, he will learn he cannot be trusted.

Throughout childhood there will be other mirrors that will show a child who he is. Teachers, friends, and caregivers will all perform this role, but a child will inevitably return to the reflection in the mirror that his parents held up for him in order to determine his goodness, importance, and self-worth.

In this book I focus on helping you to create a new mirror, one that reflects who you really are as opposed to how your parents or other primary caretakers defined you. Through a process I call Mirror Therapy you will be able to raise your self-esteem, improve your self-image (including your body image), quiet your inner critic, and heal your shame. Although this program is called Mirror Therapy, it involves a lot more than looking in the mirror. Certainly it is not based on the overly simplistic idea, depicted in an old *Saturday Night Live* skit, of looking into a mirror and repeating affirmations like "I'm good enough," "I'm smart enough," and "People like me." Instead, it is a holistic approach based on important psychological concepts, techniques, and beliefs.

I call my program Mirror Therapy for several reasons:

• The mirror symbolizes our identity.

- Parental neglect, emotional abuse, and smothering all have a negative (mirroring) effect on a child's developing identity—his or her self-concept, sense of self, and self-esteem.

- Parental emotional abuse and deprivation also have a negative effect on a child's body image and body awareness. Thus, what the child (and later, the adult) sees when he or she looks in the mirror is distorted.

- Parental emotional abuse creates in a child a negative internal judge or critic, which acts as a warped lens that distorts reality.

- The practice of *mirroring* is a fundamental aspect of parenting and is absolutely necessary if a child is to grow into a healthy adult with a strong sense of self and high self-esteem.

- Mirror Therapy involves exercises and practices using mirrors as aids to reducing shame and raising self-esteem.

- Children mirror parents' behavior.

This method focuses on how the negative view or judgment of an emotionally abusive parent defines a child's self-image; how neglect causes a child to feel worthless and unlovable; and how emotional smothering causes a child to be unable to establish a separate self from his or her parents. Even though I created Mirror Therapy especially for the many who were emotionally abused or neglected as children, it can work for anyone who suffers from low self-esteem, a poor self-image, or a powerful inner critic, or is riddled with unhealthy shame. This includes people who were physically or sexually abused.

By taking in the information in this book and by completing the exercises, you have an opportunity to reject the distorted images you received from your emotionally abusive or neglectful parents once and for all. You have the opportunity to replace these distorted images with a more accurate reflection of who you really are. I call these two processes "Shattering Your Parental Mirror" and "Creating a New Mirror." I encourage you to take this opportunity. While you cannot reverse all the damage caused by abusive or neglectful parents, you can regain much of the sense of goodness, strength, and wisdom that is your birthright.

Mirror Therapy Assignments

In addition to various exercises throughout the book, I also offer you Mirror Therapy assignments at the end of each chapter. These assignments will help you to focus on important feelings and issues that may arise as you read the book.

MIRROR THERAPY ASSIGNMENT #1

This week take the time to notice how often you criticize yourself—whether it is because you did not perform the way you expected or because you are not happy with the way you look. Also notice how often you feel exposed, unworthy, or fearful that others will discover how flawed you actually are. If you like, record how often you are self-critical, the types of criticism you notice, and how often you feel shamed and what triggers that shame.

2

The Seven Types of Negative Parental Mirrors

"Sticks and stones may break my bones but words will never hurt me," I was taught; one more lie among many. In truth words penetrate the unlidded ear and land in the spirit. Words carry hatred and passion and love and fear. Words have the power to shoot down or raise up. Sharp cutting words can whirl for years afterward like the rotating blades of a lawn mower.

—LOUISE M. WISECHILD, *The Mother I Carry*

DURING MY MANY YEARS of practice and study I have observed seven common types of negative parental mirrors. These include:

1. The "I Am Unlovable" Mirror. When parents are neglectful or do not have time for their child, they send the message that the child is unwanted or unlovable.

2. The "I Am Worthless" Mirror. When children are physically or emotionally rejected or abandoned by their parents, the message they receive is that they are worthless.

3. The "I Am Nothing without My Parent" Mirror. When parents are overprotective or emotionally smothering, they send the message that their child is helpless without them.

4. The "I Am Powerless" Mirror. When parents are overly controlling or tyrannical, they cause their child to feel powerless.

29

5. The "I Am Never Good Enough" Mirror. When parents are perfectionistic, they give their children the message that they only have value if they meet their parents' expectations—which is rare or never.

6. The "I Am Bad" or "I Am Unacceptable" Mirror. When parents are verbally abusive, hypercritical, or excessively shaming, the message they send to their child is that he or she is a bad person or is unacceptable.

7. The "I Don't Matter" Mirror. When parents are self-absorbed or narcissistic, the message they give their children is that their needs are not important and that they do not matter.

In this chapter I will address in detail the seven types of emotionally abusive and neglectful parents. I will also describe the parental mirror each of these parents holds up and the emotional damage to a child's self-image and self-esteem that is caused by each type of parenting. As you read these descriptions, notice which ones you identify with the most. Note that your parent or parents may fit into more than one category, and that you may have suffered from more than one type of emotional abuse. For example, parents who are overly critical are also often perfectionistic. Also note that there are similarities between some of the different types of emotional abuse. For instance, being neglected and being abandoned can have a similar effect on a child.

The Neglectful or Inadequate Parent
Parental Mirror: "You Are Unlovable"

Unlike other forms of childhood abuse, the damage caused by neglectful or inadequate parents has more to do with what they *didn't* do than with what they *did* do to their children.

An infant learns that she is wanted and loved by watching the smiling faces of her parents as they gaze adoringly into her eyes. A toddler learns that she is loved by the way her father loves to swoop her up in his arms and by the way her mother loves to hold her close. A preschooler learns that she is loved by seeing her mother smile as the child begins to explore the world. A grammar school child learns that she is loved when her parents scold her for doing something she shouldn't, but minutes later forgive her as they engage her in another more appropriate activity. An older child is reminded that she is loved when her parents brag about her to her grandparents—even though she only got Cs on her report card.

Children learn that they are loved by the way their parents look at them, by how much their parents want to hug them and hold them, and by how they discipline them. When a child is not looked at with loving eyes, he comes to believe he is not loved. When his parents don't seem to want to hug him or hold him, he comes to believe he must not be lovable. And when his parents' affection is taken away whenever he does something they disapprove of, he comes to believe that his lovability is contingent upon his actions and deeds.

When I first met Susan I was struck by her robotic movements and her unexpressive face. As she spoke matter-of-factly about why she had sought therapy, I also noted that her voice seemed to lack any emotion. Even before I learned more about her childhood, I could already tell that she had been severely traumatized in some way and that, in response to the trauma, she had shut down emotionally.

Although Susan had blocked out a great deal of her childhood, eventually we unearthed the truth. Susan had been severely neglected when she was a child. From an older sister she learned that as a toddler she had been left alone in her crib for hours at a time. Her diapers were seldom changed and many times she went to sleep hungry. When Susan got older her parents would often go out drinking at night and leave her all alone, and she remembered that many times there was no food in the house. Her mother was far more concerned about pleasing her father than she was about taking care of her children, and Susan rarely remembered her mother hugging or kissing her. Her father was sometimes affectionate toward Susan, but usually only after he'd had a few drinks. Then he'd put her on his lap and tickle her until she cried.

As an adult, Susan was unable to experience real love. She had a few friends and some lovers, but she could not sustain an ongoing relationship. She found it impossible to trust people and couldn't believe anyone could really care about her. If someone was nice to her, she assumed the person must want something from her. She always managed to find a way to push people away—either by being overly critical of them or by being too aloof. In general, Susan felt alone in the world and was afraid she'd always be alone. She knew there was something missing inside her and that she desperately needed help.

By neglecting her daughter in such a severe way, Susan's mother had sent her the message that she was unlovable. As children tend to blame themselves for their parents' neglect and mistreatment, it was the only conclusion Susan could come to.

Your parents need not have ignored your physical needs in order for you to have felt neglected. This is how Megan described her neglectful mother: "My mother hardly ever touched me as I was growing up. She didn't hug me or hold me. And she didn't praise me or encourage me. In fact, she hardly took an interest in me. I was just a responsibility to her—a burden really—someone she was supposed to take care of, someone she was supposed to love. But I don't know if she knew how to love. She knew how to do motherly things, like cooking and making sure my clothes were clean, but she never cared about my feelings or my emotional needs."

Inadequate Parents

Many parents neglect their children because they are simply incapable of being good parents. A person with low self-esteem will feel fearful and inadequate about being a parent and may be so afraid of making a mistake that she doesn't do much parenting at all. Or she may be so afraid of losing her children's love that she becomes too lenient. In other situations, the parent may be so overwhelmed with her own unmet needs or problems that she cannot focus on her children. Some may even look to their children for emotional support. The inadequate, immature parent often communicates to her children that she needs them to encourage and protect her, or to take care of her and boost her ego.

This was the case with Jackie. By the time she was five years old, she had already taken on the role of parent to her mother. Jackie's mother cried often—usually about Jackie's father, who had divorced her when Jackie was three—or about her own mother and her own neglectful childhood. Jackie would wipe away her mother's tears and tell her things would be okay.

To make matters worse, whenever Jackie became upset with her mother (rightfully so, because her mother neglected her so much), her mother would start to cry and say things like "I know you think I am a horrible mother" or "You're just punishing me because I don't make you the center of my universe." Because of this Jackie came to believe that it was selfish of her to expect that her own needs should be met.

Greg's mother was completely overwhelmed with life. She didn't seem to be able to function on her own without her husband or her son's support. Greg's father was frequently away at work as a traveling salesman, and his mother stayed in bed most of the time he was away, complaining of severe headaches. Instead of getting up in the morning to make Greg's breakfast, she would smile sweetly when he came into her bedroom in the morning and ask him if he minded getting her a cup of tea and some toast. Greg attempted to compensate for his mother's personality deficiencies by solving her problems. Whenever she complained to him about not being able to get up to do the housework or the grocery shopping, Greg volunteered to do it for her. When she worried that his father might be seeing other women when he was on the road, Greg reassured her that his father loved her and that he wouldn't do such a thing. When she worried about losing her figure, he assured her that she was beautiful.

Many children with alcoholic parents are burdened with the request—spoken or unspoken—to "take care of me." These children find it necessary to make excuses for their parents' behavior, assist them when they are drunk and falling down, and even get them medical help.

Diana was the oldest child in an alcoholic family. From the time she was seven years old her parents left her in charge of her three younger siblings while they went to the bar at night. Later on, in her adolescence, her mother stopped drinking due to serious medical problems, so it became Diana's job to drive her father to the bar and wait for him to come out so he wouldn't get picked up for drunk driving.

The Mirror Neglectful Parents Hold Up to Their Children

You no doubt have seen news reports on the orphans in countries such as Hungary and Romania who stand or sit in their cribs looking emaciated and forlorn. Many of these children rock back and forth to comfort themselves. The reason they are in such bad shape is not because they are not being fed adequately; it is because they are not being held. An infant or child who is severely deprived of emotional nurturing, even though physically well cared for, can fail to thrive and eventually die. There is even a name for this condition. It is called *marasmus*. Physical nurturing is so important that even after these children are adopted by well-meaning American families, they continue to suffer from severe problems, such as an inability to form an emotional bond with their parents, extreme acting out, and rage, depression, and radically low self-esteem.

Less severe forms of early emotional deprivation usually result in babies who grow into anxious and insecure children who are slow to develop or have low self-esteem. A child who is physically or emotionally neglected will tend to be either extremely needy or extremely defensive. He or she may either exhibit clinging behavior and dependency or be unable to emotionally bond with others, as was the case with Susan. Child neglect often leads to aggressive behavior in children and continues into adulthood if not treated.

EXERCISE: IDENTIFYING THE WAYS YOU WERE NEGLECTED

Put a checkmark beside each item that describes how you were treated by your parents or other caregivers. My parent or parents:

1. Ignored me or did not respond to my needs when I was an infant or toddler, including leaving me in a crib or playpen too long or not changing my diapers.

2. Didn't feed me or fed me food that was inadequate or inappropriate to a child's nutritional needs. (This does not apply if your parents were impoverished.)

3. Forced me to feed myself before I was able or to eat solid food, or before I was able to chew or digest properly.

4. Did not provide me with adequate clothing, such as a warm coat in the winter.

5. Did not bathe me regularly or wash my clothes.

6. Ignored my physical needs; did not provide me with medical or dental care when needed.

7. Did not provide me physical nurturing, such as holding, or did not comfort me when I was upset.

8. Frequently left me alone for days or weeks in the care of others.

9. Left me alone with an irresponsible or abusive caretaker.

10. On more than one occasion forgot to pick me up at the movies or after school.

11. Forced me to live in an uninhabitable place (drafty, unclean, unsafe).

12. Did not get out of bed to take care of my needs.

13. Did not allow me to leave my room or my home for long hours, days, or weeks.

14. Neglected me because they were alcohol abusers or drug users.

The Abandoning or Rejecting Parent

PARENTAL MIRROR: "YOU ARE WORTHLESS"

Some parents abandon their children *physically* through death, prolonged illness, or divorce (leaving the home and seldom if ever seeing them again), or by shipping them off to boarding school. Other parents abandon their children *emotionally* (by being emotionally unavailable, by punishing their children with silence or rejection). Both forms of abandonment are devastating to a child, usually creating emotional scars that do not heal without professional intervention.

Children who are physically abandoned are particularly wounded because they often feel as if they have no value. This is how my client Nancy described her feelings about being abandoned by her parents. "I felt like my parents threw me away, like some worthless garbage." Nancy's parents got a divorce when she was four years old and sent her to live with her grandparents ("just until they each got settled in their new jobs and new lives"). Her grandmother was very strict; Nancy missed her parents terribly and could not understand why they had abandoned her. Her mother came to see her once in a while and always promised to take her to live with her soon. Each time her mother left, Nancy felt abandoned all over again. She would lock herself in her room and cry for hours—certain that she had done something wrong to make her mother abandon her like that. Occasionally her father called but always had some excuse as to why he couldn't visit. Nancy became convinced that her parents had rejected her because she hadn't been a good daughter. She became very insecure, fearing that her grandmother would reject her as well. This made her try hard to be a perfect child, but since this was impossible, she began feeling like a worthless failure whenever she made a mistake or disappointed her grandmother.

Some parents find parenting too demanding or difficult. They resolve their dilemma by abandoning the burden of parenting, leaving their children solely in the care of a nanny or babysitters, sending them off to boarding school, or giving them away. Parents who abandon their children often rationalize their actions by saying that the child is better off without them or, in the case of boarding school, that they are providing him or her with the best opportunities money can buy. But their real intention is to be free of child care.

Parents who escape into alcohol, drugs, sleep, television, or books also abandon their children because they are essentially not there emotionally. Jennifer told me the painful story of how it felt to be raised by a mother who was emotionally detached from her. "My mother is just never present. Even if she is in the same room with me

I can't really feel her. I just can't connect with her. When I was a child it was extremely painful to be around her because I always felt so empty and alone in her presence. She didn't take an interest in anything I did or listen to anything I had to say. She would just look at me with a blank stare when I tried to talk to her. She reminded me of a ghost sometimes, kind of floating around. Most of the time she had her head stuck in a book, off in some fantasy world. In many ways I feel like I never had a mother."

Parents who are so tied up with their work or interests that they have no time for their children are, in effect, abandoning them. Often parents abandon their children because they are unable or unwilling to spend time with them. Parents who have professions that take them away from home, such as truck driving or traveling sales, are often unable to fulfill their responsibilities as a parent. Although this usually cannot be helped, the abandonment the child feels is no less poignant.

Many fathers abandon their children when they get divorced from the children's mother. They make all kinds of excuses for cutting off their ties with their children, including that their mother is demanding too much child support, or that the father needed to move out of the area for a job, but the fact is, the children feel abandoned.

Psychological Abandonment: Rejection as Abandonment

Some parents simply don't want to bother with their children, which they make very clear by their actions. Whenever their child needs help with his homework, help making a decision, or someone to listen to his problems, the parent says something like, "Can't you see I'm busy? Don't bother me with these things," or, "Go ask your father to help you," or even, "I don't want to deal with your problems." When a parent puts the child off or passes the buck to the other parent, the child senses his parent's lack of love and concern for him. Other parents communicate this same message more subtly by allowing their children to do whatever they want, but in their lenience they too are not taking an interest in their children's activities.

Parents can also show how they feel about a child by their sins of omission, such as forgetting a child's birthday, neglecting to give him gifts, buying gifts that he clearly does not want, or failing to make positive comments about him (particularly when he has done something outstanding).

Although a great deal of parental abandonment is unintentional or a result of inadequacies or selfishness on their part, some abandonment is intentional. Downplaying a child's success or saying something negative about him to someone who has just complimented him can be a way of intentionally hurting his feelings.

Some parents routinely abandon their children as a form of discipline, such as when a parent gives a child the "silent treatment" when he disapproves of what the child is doing. Rejecting parents use their power and importance to their children to control them. Children are so attached to and dependent on their parents that the loss of the support of a parent can be devastating.

When my mother was upset with me, she would routinely stop talking to me. We lived in a very small apartment, so it was difficult for us not to cross each other's path. Nevertheless, my mother would walk right past me or even sit in the same room without looking at me or saying a word. If I spoke to her she would ignore me. Sometimes she wouldn't talk to me for days. I would have to beg for her forgiveness for whatever transgression I had committed, but she still would not talk to me until she was ready. This left me feeling utterly abandoned.

My mother also used the threat of abandonment to control me. When I did something that upset her, she would say, "If you don't start minding me I'm going to send you to a convent." This is a common tactic by some abandoning, rejecting parents.

In the heat of anger or frustration some parents tell their children things like "If I had to do it all over again, I wouldn't have gotten married to your father and had you kids." While parents can sometimes secretly think these things, these thoughts should definitely be kept private, because they are correctly interpreted by the child as outright rejections. Some parents actually say these kinds of things to intentionally hurt their child.

The Mirror Held Up by Abandoning and Rejecting Parents

The secure child is nourished by the confidence that her relationship with her parents is strong and enduring and that nothing she does will make her parents abandon her. When a child does not have this inner certainty, her life is marked by it. Children who are routinely abandoned or rejected, whether intentionally or not, tend to suffer from extreme insecurity and feelings of worthlessness. They often become very upset when their parents leave to go somewhere, convinced that their parents will never return. This insecurity and fear often continues into adulthood, resulting in insecure adults who are clingy with their adult partners or who are afraid to be alone.

This was the case with Nina, who came to see me because she was being physically abused by her husband. As is the case with many abused women, Nina stayed in the relationship because she was horrified of being alone. "I know I should leave my husband but I'm so afraid of being all alone. At least now I have someone who needs me. Yes, he is possessive and jealous but there's something I like about that—it makes me feel like he likes being with me. My parents never did. They were always going out and leaving me all alone with some babysitter, and I never knew when they'd be coming back. I remember standing at the front window, watching them drive away and crying my eyes out because I thought they were gone for good. Even when they were home I never felt like they enjoyed being with me. They just seemed to tolerate me, and I was always doing something that upset or disappointed them."

Abandonment creates insecurity, self-obsession, and the tendency to turn anger against oneself and to idealize others. These feelings fester beneath the surface, where they interfere with self-image and the forming of healthy relationships. Adults who have been abandoned as children tend to lack the confidence to reach their true potential. They also have difficulty delaying gratification, and their low self-worth causes them to go for the quick fix (they eat the chocolate cake because they need it now, forfeiting the chance to have the body they desire).

Abandonment can also create self-loathing. Tammy hated herself. She hated how she looked, but it went far deeper than that. She hated who she was. "When I look in the mirror I feel so disgusted. I just can't stand the person I have become." Tammy came to me because she was a cutter (a person who has an uncontrollable compulsion to cut herself). Research has shown that 50 percent of cutters have been sexually abused, and so my immediate assumption was that perhaps this was the cause of Tammy's self-loathing. But as far as Tammy could remember, she had never been molested. Instead, it appeared that her self-loathing was caused by the deep sense of abandonment she felt concerning her father. Even though Tammy's father came home from work every day and spent the evening with his family, Tammy felt horribly abandoned by him. "I don't remember my father ever hugging me," she explained in one of our sessions. "In fact, he seldom ever looked at me. When I came close to him he actually backed away, as if he was repulsed by me. It made me feel so ugly and so terrible about myself. I figured I must be a disgusting human being for my own father to be so revolted by me."

The Smothering, Possessive, or Intrusive Parent

Parental Mirror: "You Are Nothing without Me"

This type of parent smothers his or her children with overprotection, guilt, rules, and demands. Many are desperate for their child's love and attention. Smothering parents are overly invested in their children, often making huge sacrifices and commitments but expecting the child's soul in return. They will often go to any length to make certain that their children do not experience the necessary separation-individuation process and have independent lives. *I want you all for myself* is the underlying theme, and the mirror the smothering parent holds up to the child is "You are nothing without me."

Mark's mother did everything for him. When he was a child she continued to cut up his food even after he was capable of doing so himself. She continued to clean his room well into high school and never required him to do any household chores.

Both his parents were overprotective to the point of smothering. They constantly warned him about the potential dangers all around him. "Don't go into the deep water, you'll drown," "Don't ever use a public toilet or you'll get a disease." They discouraged him from roller-skating because they were afraid he'd fall and break a bone, and they didn't let him take the training wheels off his bicycle until he was seven years old.

This overprotectiveness doomed Mark to become an under-achiever as an adult. His parents' negative views of life became a self-fulfilling prophecy, and because his mother had done everything for him, he never learned how to assume responsibility for himself or his possessions. His lack of survival knowledge was embarrassing to him, and he tended to neglect his health and his physical appearance.

Smothering parents emotionally and sometimes physically engulf their children. They can be controlling, overbearing, or simply ever-present in their child's life. This engulfment discourages independence and breeds unhealthy dependence. It also can create an attitude of hopelessness and powerlessness on a child's part. If everything is done for you, as it was in Mark's case, or if you are discouraged from trying things on your own, how can you know what you are capable of?

There are several types of smothering, possessive parents:

- Those who are motivated primarily by fear (fear of something bad happening to their child) as with Mark's parents

- Those who need to control their children

- Those who want their children to think, feel, and do just as they do

- Those who do not feel separate from their children and therefore do not want their children to be independent from them

- Those who fear being alone and therefore attempt to tie their children to them by making them dependent on them

- Those who see their children as reflections of themselves—narcissistic parents

- Those who use their child to satisfy needs that should be satisfied by other adults

While people who were neglected or abandoned often feel invisible, those who were smothered often feel the opposite. They tend to feel overly scrutinized—so much so that they wish for a place to hide from the ever-present gaze of their parent. Often the look is that of a disapproving parent who is just waiting for them to do something wrong. Other times the look is that of a worried parent who fears someone or something will hurt the child. Whatever the intention of the look, the result is that children who are smothered and engulfed often have a difficult time discovering who they are apart from their parent and in separating from that gaze. "Even when I was out of my mother's sight I still felt her looking at me," my client Samantha told me. "It was as if her eyes followed me wherever I went. As a matter of fact, I still feel those eyes on me today—judging my every move." Still another client, Monica, explained it like this: "It is as if my eyes are my mother's eyes. I see everything from the context of whether or not she would approve of what I am doing, or whether she would approve of a person I am with. It's like I'm never really on my own, to make my own decisions, to make my own mistakes."

The reason Samantha and Monica experience life this way is that their mothers discouraged their individuality. Both mothers were overly invested in their daughters' becoming replicas of themselves. They wanted them to think, feel, and act just the way they did; any differences were viewed as threatening.

Smothering parents often have difficulty seeing their children as separate human beings with their own needs and feelings. They often assume they know what their child needs and insist they know what their child is thinking. This mind reading can be especially damaging to a child because it makes him feel intruded upon and separates him from his own private world. This is how my client Jordan explained it: "My dad always thought he knew what I was thinking and feeling. Instead of asking me what I was feeling, he'd tell me. I hated it when he did that. It was like I couldn't even have my own private thoughts without him intruding upon them. What really bothered me was that sometimes he was right. That really freaked me out. It was like he had the power to read my mind. I had no place to hide."

Some smothering parents insist that their children adopt their values. This is often true of highly religious parents, but it also occurs in the homes of people who come from other countries and have maintained the old country's traditions. I have had many clients from Europe, South America, and Mexico whose parents were overly smothering, including my client Lupe, whose parents came from Central Mexico.

"My dad acted as if he owned me—body and soul. I had absolutely no say in what I wanted to do. Everything was dictated by what was proper for a young girl. When I was little I had to wear these frilly dresses, which I hated. I was always stuck in the kitchen with my mother and aunts and could never play games out in the backyard like my brothers were allowed to do. As I got older I still had no choices. I was told I had to go to a Catholic high school, that I had to take certain classes, and that I couldn't date until I was eighteen—and then only if my older brother went along as a chaperone."

When Lupe finished high school she wanted to go on to college, but her father insisted they didn't have enough money to send a girl to school when they still had two more boys coming up. Even when Lupe got a college scholarship, her father insisted that she stay home to take care of her ailing grandmother. Lupe quietly obeyed her dad. "I know American girls would have fought for what they wanted, but you just don't disagree with my dad—not in our culture. That would have meant I don't love him and it would have been like turning my back on everything I was raised to believe in."

When Lupe first came to see me she was twenty-five years old. She had fallen in love with a white man, and she knew her father would never accept him. "I know what I need to do. I need to say good-bye to Tom. I just wish I didn't love him so much. I've tried walking away, but we work together and seeing him every day causes me almost unbearable pain. But I can't hurt my father like this. I just can't."

This would be a difficult situation for anyone, but for someone who had never been allowed to make her own choices the situation was particularly daunting. Lupe had started suffering from horrible stomach pains and she was missing a lot of work because of it. "I guess

I'm just going to have to quit my job. That way I won't have to see Tom. I don't know what else to do." It didn't occur to Lupe that her health was being affected by her inability to stand up to her father and do what was right for herself.

The Possessive Parent

The possessive parent wants to control, own, and consume her child. She begins when her child is an infant, overprotecting him, holding him so close that he may feel suffocated. When the child reaches the age where he wants to begin to explore the world separate from his parent, the possessive parent feels threatened and clings to her child even tighter. This need to possess can continue throughout childhood, causing the parent to feel jealous of anything and everyone that threatens to take him away. For example, the parent may discourage her child from making friends by always finding fault with each of his playmates. Instead of beginning to loosen the reins a little as he becomes older and more mature, she may become even more strict, insisting on knowing at all times where her child is going and with whom. When he begins to take an interest in dating, the possessive parent may become especially threatened and may either forbid her child to date or make him feel that no one is good enough for him.

Some fathers and stepfathers become very possessive of their daughters. This can come out of a reluctance to acknowledge that one day their "little girl" will grow up and marry. But other times it arises out of the fact that the father is sexually aroused by his daughter and doesn't want any other man to have her. This kind of father will typically forbid his daughter to date and will be horrified if she wears anything that he feels is the slightest bit revealing.

Emotional Incest

Other parents become what is called emotionally incestuous with their children. These parents desperately crave their child's love and attention. Their message to their children, although usually unspoken, is:

"Above all, always be available to me." Parents who have been divorced or widowed often attempt to replace the lost spouse with their own child. If a parent treats his or her child like a confidante or friend instead of maintaining a parent/child relationship, this is a form of emotional incest. It is not a child's role to make parents feel good or to listen to their problems.

Emotionally incestuous parents turn to their children to satisfy needs that should be satisfied by other adults—namely intimacy, companionship, romantic stimulation, advice, problem solving, ego fulfillment, and/or emotional release.

Emotional incest can take many forms. On one end of the spectrum the parent treats the child more like a buddy or a peer. She either becomes childlike herself and may even interfere with her child's social life (by wanting to hang out with the child's friends) or she expects her child to act like an adult friend who will talk to her about adult issues and feelings. She may also emotionally "dump" on her child by talking about her problems to the child. This can include complaining to the child about the other parent. Sometimes both parents dump on a child in a way that puts the child in the middle.

On the other end of the spectrum, the parent turns to a child of the opposite sex for the intimacy and companionship one would normally expect to find in a romantic relationship. There is often a flirtatious, teasing quality in this relationship and in many cases, an undercurrent of sexuality.

The Mirror That Smothering or Possessive Parents Hold Up to Their Children

Smothering or possessive parents do not allow their children the space to grow and develop their unique personalities. Because they do not allow their children to separate from them, they restrict and limit their children's potential to make something of themselves in the world. Because adult children of smothering parents are overly concerned about their parents being devastated when they leave home, many do not do so. The ones who physically leave home often remain emotionally bound to their parents.

Donna's parents discouraged her from leaving home by warning her of all the dangers there were for young women. Every evening her father would read some horror story in the local paper about a woman who had gone missing or had been raped. Her parents also stressed that young girls had no business going out to dance clubs. "These young girls are asking for trouble," they'd say. Donna actually got up the courage to move out when she was twenty-two, right after she graduated from college. She and her friend Mary found an apartment together. But she soon felt compelled to move back home. "Mary went out almost every night and I felt lonely and scared in that apartment all alone. She tried to get me to go out with her to the clubs, but I really didn't like it. I knew my dad didn't like me going there and that it made my parents worry about me. Besides, my dad told me that my mother had been really depressed ever since I left home."

A smothering parent assumes that her child's mistakes will trap him for life, and so she will try to manage her child's life in such a way that the child will accept his parents' attitudes about the world. We saw this happening with Lupe earlier in the chapter. The problem is that the parent's behavior prevents an adult child from developing his own attitudes and beliefs. Although a smothering parent may only be trying to protect her child from harm and disappointment, her attempts may actually emotionally cripple the child later in life, causing him to fear venturing out on his own or trying new things.

If a child identifies with his parents' overprotective attitude, as we saw with the example of Mark, he will live his life in fear, doomed to being an underachiever. If he is unable to take risks out of fear of getting hurt, he will never experience the joy of accomplishment and the pride of reaching his potential. This will inevitably cause him to feel like a failure and to suffer from low self-esteem. When parents transmit a lack of confidence in their children's ability to get along in the world, or constantly warn them of how people are untrustworthy, they often create a self-fulfilling prophecy in which the child grows up overwhelmed with insecurity or expecting people to disappoint, hurt, or take advantage of him.

Because their parents' needs cancel their own, adult children of smothering or possessive parents are often unable to discover what their own needs are, and many grow up to passively accept even unacceptable behavior instead of asserting themselves. Many who were smothered in this way end up also being controlled by their partners, bosses, or other significant people in their lives.

The Overly Controlling, Tyrannical Parent

PARENTAL MIRROR: "YOU ARE POWERLESS"

Lorraine is an attractive woman with large, dark eyes, flawless skin, and a luscious mouth. She was once considered voluptuous but is now extremely overweight. But what stands out the most about Lorraine is that she talks and acts like a little girl. At nearly forty years old she has the mannerisms of a young child. Although she is quite intelligent, she frequently appears confused and cannot easily understand instructions from her employers, which has cost her more than one job. Why does Lorraine behave the way she does? She is still suffering from the emotional abuse she experienced as a child at the hands of her mother.

When Lorraine was a child she was expected to act like an adult. Her mother insisted that she and her sisters take responsibility for cleaning the entire house while she was at work. This wouldn't have been so bad, except that her mother was a perfectionist. The girls could never do anything right. Lorraine remembers one time when her mother told her to scrub the kitchen floor, even though she was only six years old.

As usual, when her mother got home from work she inspected the house, looking for anything out of place or left undone. When she found scuff marks on the kitchen floor, she became furious. She yelled at Lorraine, calling her "a stupid good-for-nothing girl who never did anything right." Lorraine was humiliated. She told her mother that she had tried and tried but was not able to get the scuff marks off. Even though it was past Lorraine's bedtime, her mother insisted that she scrub the floor until the marks were completely gone. This took hours. By the time the marks were gone Lorraine's fingers were bruised and bleeding.

Lorraine still remembers how helpless and hopeless she felt as she desperately tried to get the scuff marks off the floor. Today, whenever a boss asks her to do something, Lorraine panics. She is so afraid of doing something wrong that she becomes frozen in fear and is unable to move. It takes her several minutes to come back to herself and by that time she has forgotten what her boss asked her to do.

The mirror that Lorraine's mother held up led Lorraine to believe that she was powerless and incapable of doing anything right. This prevented Lorraine from developing self-efficacy and positive self-esteem. It also stunted her emotional growth, leaving her feeling like a perpetual child, overwhelmed by authority figures and responsibility.

The tyrannical parent has a cruel and inflexible style of parenting. Often every member of the household, including her spouse, is expected to blindly obey her and grant all her wishes, no matter how outrageous. This type of parent usually believes strongly in rules and obedience and that the authority of parents should never be questioned. They attempt to dominate their children completely, needing to feel in control over others in order to feel powerful and important.

Sometimes this controlling behavior is dictated by perfectionism, as was the case with Lorraine's mother. Other times parents are motivated by a sheer need to dominate, often because they were dominated by their own parents. They are often passing on the same behavior to their children and ventilating the anger they could not express to their own parents.

A child growing up with an overly controlling parent hears a barrage of commands, orders, and suggestions about anything and everything, including what foods to eat, how to eat them, what clothes to wear, what classes to take in school, or what type of person to date.

Many children feel tyrannized by their parents' moods. "My father's moods fluctuated constantly," my client Tyrone told me during his first session. "We'd be getting along just fine and then suddenly, for no apparent reason, he would blow up and yell at me about something. Then he'd insist I do something stupid, like go out and mow the lawn, even though it had just been mowed a few days before."

The Mirror Controlling or Tyrannical Parents Hold Up

Children who grow up with a tyrant for a parent will feel weakened from their encounters with their parents and will inevitably have deep emotional scars from the experience. Like Lorraine, they will doubt their abilities and may feel unbearable pressure when asked to do something, particularly when an authority figure is doing the asking. They often feel stupid, inadequate, and incompetent, and these feelings usually discourage them from trying new things or taking risks.

The following e-mail is an example of how controlling parents can break a child's spirit.

> Dear Beverly,
> I have read your book *The Emotionally Abused Woman* and have learned a lot from it. I am a twenty-eight-year-old woman who is still living with my parents. My mother is verbally abusive and there has been an incident of physical abuse. I feel so ashamed to still be living at home at my age, but I don't have enough money after my monthly bills are paid to seriously save to move out. I left college a year ago because of personal and financial reasons. My parents are extremely disappointed that I didn't finish, and remind me of that often. I quit college because it would have meant quitting my job and being even more dependent on my parents.
> The situation continues to get worse. I cannot stand being around my parents. All my life I have felt inferior. I want to leave but I don't have the money. I feel I can't take any more. But my parents say if I would just listen to them, my life would be better. Are they right?

Just as too much physical force can break a child's bones, too much control can break a child's spirit and fracture his psyche. It can cause a splintering of self, causing a child to disown some parts of himself and to inflate others.

Children growing up with a tyrannical parent often become what is referred to by professionals as *hypervigilant*, meaning they develop extraordinary abilities to notice any warning signs of an impending attack. They learn to recognize subtle changes in the facial expressions and voice and body language of others as signals of anger, intoxication, dissociation, or sexual arousal. When they sense danger, they attempt to protect themselves by either avoiding or placating the other person. In addition, children with a tyrannical parent usually carry around a great deal of repressed anger—repressed because they cannot afford to admit they have it, much less risk expressing it.

The Perfectionistic Parent
PARENTAL MIRROR: "YOU ARE NEVER GOOD ENOUGH"

Perfectionistic parents are often driven by a fear of disorder, uncleanliness, or flaws. They tend to put a great value on appearances, status, and material possessions, or on what others will think. Many feel strongly that anything short of perfection is failure. Consequently, they are also domineering and tyrannical when it comes to what they expect from their children.

Rod's father expected him to excel in everything he attempted. During high school and college, his father insisted he bring home all As, be class president every year, and shine on the football field. Needless to say, this was a heavy burden. Whenever Rod made a mistake, his father would always say to him, "Get on the stick, Wilson." Whenever he complained about being tired or showed any weakness, his father would say, "There's no room for whiners at the top."

By the time Rod graduated from college, he was emotionally numb. "I pushed myself so hard all my life that I don't even know who I am. When I look in the mirror I don't even recognize who I see."

We've all heard of perfectionistic parents who push their children to excel in a particular sport, in academics, or in other endeavors. These children are given the powerful message (sometimes spoken, often unspoken) that they only have value if they perform to their parents' satisfaction. Oftentimes this is because the parent is living through his child, trying to make up for his own lost dreams.

Perfectionistic parents tend to have disdain for flaws of any kind. This makes them especially critical of their children's appearance. "My mother was always concerned about the way I looked," my client Veronica told me. "She hated my teeth, which were crooked like my father's, so she taught me how to smile without showing my teeth. She couldn't wait until I was old enough to get braces, but even then she seemed to be embarrassed by the fact that I had to wear them."

Veronica's mother's concern about her appearance understandably made her very self-conscious. "I thought I was a real ugly duckling," she confided. "I thought everyone had the same reaction to my teeth and later my braces as my mother did—that they couldn't stand to look at me. Today, even though I have nice straight teeth, I still smile with my mouth closed and put my hand in front of my mouth a lot."

The Mirror Perfectionistic Parents Hold Up to Their Children

Instead of receiving encouragement and support from their parents, children of perfectionistic parents tend to receive only criticism, demands, and sometimes ridicule. Consequently, they often grow up feeling inadequate, incapable, awkward, or inept. Since they receive little praise or constructive guidance, their self-esteem is usually very low, and they have little faith in their own abilities. They are often overwhelmed with anxiety whenever they have to perform in any way, and this sets them up for failure. In addition, people raised by perfectionistic parents tend to suffer from any or all of the following problems:

- A sense that they are valued for what they *do* instead of for who they *are* (*doing* versus *being*)
- A tendency to be self-critical, never satisfied with themselves or their performance
- A tendency to doubt themselves and to second-guess
- An inability to identify and express their emotions
- Compulsive behaviors (extreme dieting, overexercising, excessive cleaning)
- Depression

Hypercritical, Shaming Parents
Parental Mirror: "You Are Bad" or
"You Are Unacceptable"

Stephen grew up feeling that both his parents didn't like him very much. "Our home was a very cold place," Stephen shared with me during our first session. "My mother didn't want to spend time with me. She said I reminded her of my father—that I was stubborn and opinionated just like he was. She always looked at me with disdain, as if to say, 'You're so miserable I don't want to be around you.'" His earliest memory is of being in a crib, screaming at the top of his lungs. He felt he had done something wrong and was being punished for it.

His father was a strict disciplinarian, and Stephen always seemed to be in trouble with him. He often shamed Stephen because Stephen didn't meet his expectations. "I tried to be perfect so I wouldn't disappoint my dad and so I wouldn't get punished, but no matter how hard I tried I never made the mark."

Stephen was a bed-wetter until age ten and felt a lot of shame about it. His mother constantly complained about having to wash his sheets. Eventually, Stephen began to view himself in the same way his parents did—as a bad kid. "Who I was, wasn't acceptable." His mother also became verbally and physically abusive toward him, especially after she and his father got a divorce. "She used to call me a loser. When my dad left it became obvious that she didn't want anything to do with me." The last time his mother beat him, he ran away from home and never returned. He was fifteen. He ended up moving in with some older boys he had befriended.

"I always felt like I was under my parents' thumb when I was at home. With my friends I felt freedom for the first time in my life. I didn't need a mother or a father—I decided I'd raise myself."

And that he did. He became very demanding of himself. He did well in his last years of high school and even went on to college, paying for his tuition by working at a grocery store as a bag boy. Stephen built a fortress around himself to prevent himself from ever getting hurt again.

When I met Stephen he couldn't cry, even though his wife was threatening to leave him. "I don't know why my wife married me in the first place. I'm just no good," he told me at our first session. The sad truth was that Stephen had pushed his wife away because he was so afraid of losing her and so convinced that he was not worthy of her.

How Parents Shame Their Children

Sometimes parents deliberately shame their children into minding without realizing the disruptive impact shame can have on the child's sense of self. Statements such as "You should be ashamed of yourself" or "Shame on you" are obvious examples. Yet, because these kinds of statements are overtly shaming, they are actually easier for the child to defend against than more subtle forms of shaming such as contempt, humiliation and public shaming. For example, behavior that is acceptable at home is suddenly seen by parents as bad when they are in public. Or a parent seems to be ashamed because a child is not adhering to certain social norms that he is completely unaware of. Such comments as "Stop that, you're embarrassing me in front of everyone" not only cause a child to feel exposed, judged, and ashamed but also burden him with his parents' shame as well.

There are many ways that parents shame their children. These include belittling, blaming, contempt, humiliation, and disabling expectations:

- *Belittling.* Comments such as "You're too old to want to be held" or "You're just a crybaby" are horribly humiliating to a child. When a parent makes a negative comparison between his child and another, such as, "Why can't you act like Tommy? Tommy isn't a crybaby," it is not only humiliating but also teaches a child to always compare himself with peers and find himself deficient.

- *Blaming.* When a child makes a mistake, such as accidentally hitting a ball through a neighbor's window, he needs to take responsibility. But many parents go way beyond teaching the child a lesson by blaming and berating their children: "You stupid idiot! You should have known better than to play so close to the house! Now I'm going to have to pay for that window. Do you think money grows on trees? I don't have enough money to constantly be cleaning up your messes!" All this accomplishes is to shame the child to such an extent that he cannot find a way to walk away from the situation with his head held high. Blaming the child like this is like rubbing his nose in the mess he made, and it produces such intolerable shame that he may be forced to deny responsibility or find ways of excusing it.

- *Contempt.* Expressions of disgust or contempt communicate absolute rejection. The look of contempt (often a sneer or a raised upper lip), especially from someone who is significant to a child, can be a devastating inducer of shame, because the child is made to feel disgusting or offensive. Having an overly critical parent, one who always finds something wrong with the child, guarantees that the child will be constantly subjected to shame. When I was a child, my mother had an extremely negative attitude toward me. Much of the time she either looked at me expectantly, as though she were saying, "What are you up to now?" or with disapproval or disgust over what I had already done. These looks were extremely shaming to me, causing me to feel that there was something terribly wrong with me.

- *Humiliation.* As Gershen Kaufman stated in his book *Shame: The Power of Caring*: "There is no more humiliating experience than to have another person who is clearly the stronger and more powerful take advantage of that power and give us a beating." I can personally attest to this. In addition to shaming me with her contemptuous looks, my mother often punished me by hitting me with the branch off a tree, and she often did this outside, in front of the neighbors. The humiliation I felt was like a deep wound to my soul.

- *Disabling expectations.* Appropriate parental expectations serve as necessary guides to behavior and are not disabling. Disabling expectations, on the other hand, involve pressuring a child to excel or perform a task, a skill, or an activity. Parents who have an inordinate need to have their children excel are likely to behave in ways that pressure a child to do more and more. According to Kaufman, when a child becomes aware of the real possibility of failing to meet parental expectations, he or she often experiences a blinding self-consciousness—the painful watching of oneself—that is very disabling. When something is expected of us in this way, attaining the goal is made harder, if not impossible.

Yet another way that parents induce shame in their children is by communicating to them that they are a disappointment. Such messages as "I can't believe you could do such a thing" or "I am deeply disappointed in you," accompanied by a disapproving tone of voice and facial expression, can crush a child's spirit.

The Mirror That Criticizing and Shaming Parents Hold Up to Their Children

Overly critical parents can destroy their child's confidence and self-esteem and devastate their self-image. Instead of motivating children, overly critical comments tend to destroy a child's will to succeed and his capacity to change, and deprive him of motivation.

Like Stephen, a child who is shamed by rejection, mockery, or expressions of disgust or contempt will often shrink from contact with others. He may seek invisibility in order to feel safe. He grows up feeling unlovable because he was taught that it was his fault that his parents did not love him, or that his acceptance was conditional—depending on whether he performed to his parents' satisfaction.

Because shame is so debilitating, it makes sense that we would do almost anything to avoid it. Human beings strive to stay in control. We are raised to believe that we are responsible for what happens to us and that we can control our own lives. When something goes wrong, we tend to feel ashamed about the fact that we have lost control of our lives. This is especially true of children, who instead of simply believing that something bad "just happened," tend to believe that they somehow caused or contributed to the events and are therefore responsible for them. Being victimized causes us to feel helpless, and it is this helplessness that leads us to feel humiliated and ashamed. As a protection against these feelings we may take personal responsibility for our own victimization.

Becoming Shame-Bound

Sometimes a child has been so severely shamed or experienced so many shame-inducing incidents that he or she becomes what is referred to as "shame-bound" or "shame-based," meaning that shame has become a dominant factor in the formation of the person's personality. Shame-based people suffer from extremely low self-esteem, feelings of worth-lessness, and self-hatred. They feel inferior, "bad," unacceptable, and different from others. They were often taught that they were worthless or bad by hearing adults say such things to them as "You are in my way," "I wish you were never born," or "You'll never amount to anything."

Shame-based people are commonly survivors of severe physical discipline, emotional abuse, neglect, and abandonment—which all send the message that the child is worthless, unacceptable, and bad. These acts also convey the message that the adult will treat you any way he or she wants because you are a worthless commodity. Many shame-based people were also humiliated for their behavior (being chastised or beaten in front of others, being told, "What's wrong with you?" or "What would your precious teacher think of you if she knew who you *really* are?"). Last but not least, shame-based people often had to endure shame-inducing traumas like child sexual abuse.

Shame-based people tend to defend against any feeling of shame with anger. Whereas most people react with anger whenever they are made to feel humiliated, devalued, or demeaned, shame-based or shame-bound people tend to be extremely sensitive and defensive. They go into rages when they feel criticized or attacked—which is often. Because they are so critical of themselves, they believe every-one else is critical of them. And because they despise themselves, they assume everyone else dislikes them. If you are shame-bound, one teasing comment or one well-intentioned criticism can send you into a rage that lasts for hours. Because you feel shamed by the other person's comment, you may spend hours making the other person feel horrible about himself by dumping shame back on him.

Another way shame-based people use anger as a defense is by attacking others before they have a chance to attack them. It's as if they are saying, "I'll show you. I'll make you feel like shit because that's what you think of me."

Shame-based people feel very vulnerable underneath all their defensiveness. If you are shame-bound, you may also use anger to keep people away from your vulnerability by raging at them. In essence you are saying, "Don't get any closer to me. I don't want you to know who I really am." This type of raging works; it drives people away or keeps them at a safe distance. Of course, this also makes you feel even worse when you realize that others are avoiding you.

Rage

Rage occurs spontaneously and naturally following shame. It serves a vital self-protective function by insulating the self against further exposure and by actively keeping others away to avoid further occurrences of shame. Extroverted children are more likely to express rage at being shamed, while introverted children often tend to keep their rage inside, more hidden from the view of others.

Humiliation can be a fertile breeding ground for hatred and for revenge-seeking. By hating one's oppressor and nursing revenge fantasies, the shamed and wounded person can salvage something of his or her dignity. To do otherwise, to give in to the power of others, may feel to some like a relinquishing of integrity and, in doing so, a loss of self-respect.

A related way that victims suppress their feelings of helplessness is by *identifying with the aggressor*. We find this phenomenon to be particularly common with boy victims. In most societies it is not acceptable for men to be perceived as victims. Because of this, boys tend to blame themselves and even convince themselves that they caused the behavior in the abusive person. The boy may also come to identify with the aggressor—that is, become like his abuser. The only way left for him to discharge his shame and aggression is to do to others what was done to him.

As Gershen Kaufman explains in *The Power of Caring*: "If rage emerges as a strategy of defense, what we will see is an individual who holds onto rage as a characterological style. This manifests itself either in hostility towards others or bitterness. Although this hostility or bitterness arises as a defense to protect the self against further experiences of shame, it becomes disconnected from its originating source and becomes a generalized reaction directed toward almost anyone who may approach."

If you recognize some or all of the examples of parental shaming listed previously, this exercise will help you further identify and process what you personally experienced as a child.

1. Make a list of experiences in childhood and adolescence that shamed you the most.

2. Write down how each of these experiences made you feel.

3. How did you react to the shaming experiences of your childhood? Did you blame yourself? Did you become angry?

4. How do you think these shaming experiences have affected your life? Write down your insights.

The Self-Absorbed or Narcissistic Parent
PARENTAL MIRROR: "YOU DON'T MATTER"
OR "YOU ARE INVISIBLE"

Some parents are egocentric, meaning that their needs, wants, and beliefs are always more important than their children's (or anyone else's for that matter). These parents have little or no sense that their disregard (active or passive) for their child is teaching her that she is not worth much. Such treatment tends to result in either self-hatred or an idealized, defensive sense of self that leads to frustration, failure, and unhappiness for the child.

My client Sara described her mother in this way: "My mother was completely self-absorbed. Everything centered around her—her needs, her interests, her ideas. Most of the time I was invisible to her. I could be in the same room with her and she wouldn't notice me. If I needed anything she acted as if it was a huge imposition. I didn't dare interrupt her when she was busy or she'd snap at me and make me feel like I was being selfish by bothering her. The only time she seemed to validate my existence was if I drew some positive attention to myself. As a little girl, if someone told me I was cute, my mother would beam with pride and make some comment about how much I looked like her. When I discovered I had a talent for music, she told me I had gotten it from her. As far as she was concerned, there was nothing I achieved on my own—it was either because I inherited it from her, because she helped me, or because she made it possible."

Like a self-absorbed parent, a narcissistic parent is only interested in what reflects on herself. Her needs are all-important; nothing and no one else counts, including her children. But narcissistic parents take self-absorption to an even greater extreme. Everything a narcissist does or experiences is seen as a reflection of self; therefore, her children are perceived as her possessions, useful to her only if they can provide something she needs—admiration from others, validation that she is a good mother, or someone who will adore her and put her on a pedestal. Narcissists enjoy the power they have as a parent and use it to build up their own shaky egos.

Mason came to see me because he wanted my help in breaking away from his mother. He was twenty-five but had been living on his own for only about six months. "When I left home my mother acted as if I'd stabbed her in the heart," Mason lamented. "All I did was what kids are supposed to do—grow up and become independent from their parents!" To make matters worse, Mason was an artist, and his mother had acted as his manager for many years, doing all the legwork of getting his paintings in galleries. "I am very grateful for all my mother has done for me, but frankly, she did it more for herself than for me. It made her feel good about herself for raising such a child prodigy, and she took most of the credit for my career. You should hear her talking about how much she did to encourage my talent as I was growing up and what hard work it was getting people to take notice of my work. Now that I'm on my own, she feels threatened. I'm showing her I don't need her, and she doesn't like it."

Mason was describing a typical narcissistic mother—chronically cold but at the same time overprotective. She invades her child's autonomy and manipulates him to conform to her wishes. She rejects all about him that she finds objectionable, putting him in the anxiety-ridden position of losing her affection if he expresses dissatisfaction.

Psychological health comes from the experience, starting in early infancy, of parental acceptance. It comes from learning that although you are not perfect, you are still worthy of love. Children need to know that all that they are—both good and bad, naughty and nice, smart and stupid—is acceptable to their parents. But children of narcissistic parents do not experience this kind of acceptance. Instead, a narcissistic parent rejects everything about her child that she finds imperfect or objectionable. She has extremely high expectations of her child and continuously works on improving him.

As Elan Golumb wrote in her classic book *Trapped in the Mirror: Adult Children of Narcissists in their Struggle for Self*, the child of a narcissist has rejection as her birthright. Because a narcissistic parent unconsciously despises himself (due to his parents' rejection of him), he cannot accept his children. His attitude—a variant of the old Groucho Marx adage "I would not join any club that would have me as its member"—becomes "I would not love any child who would have me as its parent." Therefore, the narcissistic parent is most demanding and deforming of the child he identifies with most strongly.

In its extreme, narcissism becomes a character disorder. Someone with narcissistic personality disorder, or NPD, as described in *The Diagnostic and Statistical Manual of Mental Disorders* (DSM-IV), has the following characteristics:

1. An inflated or grandiose sense of self-importance (for example, exaggerates own abilities and achievements)

2. A preoccupation with fantasies of unlimited success, fame, power, beauty, and perfect love (uncritical adoration)

3. A belief that he or she is special and unique and can only be appreciated and understood by other special or high-status people

4. Requires excessive admiration

5. A sense of entitlement, that is, unreasonable expectations of being treated especially favorable or automatic granting of his or her own wishes

6. Exploitative in his or her interpersonal relationships; that is, takes advantage of others to achieve his or her own needs

7. A lack of empathy for others; is unwilling or unable to recognize or identify with the feelings and needs of others

8. Is often envious of others or believes that others are envious of him or her

9. Arrogance or haughtiness in behavior and attitudes

In addition, those with NPD or strong narcissistic traits will exhibit the following: a tendency to feel rage with little objective cause; a readiness to treat people with cool indifference as punishment for hurtful treatment or as an indication of the fact that they have no current use for the person; a tendency toward severe feelings of inferiority, shame, and emptiness; a need to be looked at and admired (exhibitionism); and a tendency to overidealize or devalue people based largely on a narrow focus.

Narcissistic parents have an investment in preventing their children from becoming separate individuals. They do not recognize that their children have their own needs, feelings, desires, and perceptions. For example, these parents believe their children should always be as happy or as miserable as they are. When a child does not share their own emotional moods, it is taken as a sign of disloyalty and insensitivity. Children of narcissists are trained to distrust the reality of their own thoughts and to allow others to think for them, because a narcissist attempts to define his children's reality. He tells them what they are feeling and thinking, often creating great confusion in the children's minds.

Any movement toward autonomy on the part of the child is greeted by the parent's pain, resentment, and anger. Children of narcissists often feel they do not have a right to exist. As Elan Golumb so eloquently stated in *Trapped in the Mirror*, "Their selves have been twisted out of their natural shape, since any movement toward independence is treated as a betrayal and something that can cause the parent irreparable harm."

The Mirror That Narcissistic Parents Hold Up to Their Children

The child of a narcissist becomes the carrier of both his parents' rejected imperfections and his parents' grandiose fantasies. This creates a self-image that is extremely contradictory—he is a miserable failure who will never accomplish anything and at the same time he is capable of total perfection and admiration. The child's inner self is treated as identical with his external behavior and the products he creates. He is barraged with criticism, which he inevitably comes to believe. On top of all this damage, the narcissistic parent frames his comments in such a way that he implicates the child's inner self. It isn't that he got a bad grade on a paper, it is that he is a failure. As a result, the child cannot be objective about what he does and cannot utilize criticism effectively. It hurts too much to take in.

As a result, children of narcissists often have serious problems with performance. Because of their fear of failure and their damaged self-esteem, they find many ways of hiding. Although adult children of narcissistic parents may achieve competence in some areas, they usually achieve only a small measure of their true potential. They are slowed down, constricted by the lack of confidence their narcissistic parents showed in them and by their own defenses against their parents' criticism, control, manipulation, and rejection.

This is how Elan Golumb describes it: "One terrible defensive outcome is to settle into an emotionally robotic existence in which they feel neither the pain of childhood nor the realization of life's pleasures. Feelingless and neutral, we defer to the parent's prohibition of our becoming a separate person."

MIRROR THERAPY ASSIGNMENT #2

1. Write down each of the negative mirrors your parents held up to you. While you may relate to many or even all of the descriptions and examples, is there one that you resonate with more than any other?

2. Write a detailed description of the way your parents treated you. Include any behavior on their part that led you to feel inadequate, incompetent, unloved, shamed, worthless, alone, or helpless.

3

Your Body as a Mirror

Self-contempt never inspires lasting change.

—JANE R. HIRSCHMANN AND CAROL H. MUNTER,
When Women Stop Hating Their Bodies

YOUR BODY IMAGE AND THE WAY YOU FEEL and care about your body are essential parts of your overall sense of self-worth and level of self-esteem. All the work you will be doing in this book will help raise your self-esteem, but in this chapter we will focus on your body image. We will begin by helping you become more aware of your body image and where your ideas about your body came from. Later on in the book, we will focus on how you can make lasting and meaningful improvements to your body image.

Body image is the view or perception that you have of your physical appearance—what it looks like to you and what you think it looks like to others. For many people, low self-esteem is caused by a negative body image, while for others low self-esteem comes first and the negative body image follows from it.

Often our bodies reflect how we feel about ourselves. What does your body say about you? In what ways does it reflect your overall sense of self-worth? Does your body say, "I feel really good about myself," or does it say, "I feel really crappy about myself"?

In addition to how you feel about yourself, your body is a reflection of many other things, including:

- How safe you feel in the world
- Your level of emotional and/or physical health
- How well you were taken care of physically and emotionally as a child
- The messages your parents passed on concerning body perfection
- The messages your parents gave you about self-care
- The messages you received from your parents (and others) about how they felt about your body

The sad truth is that even if you have a near-perfect body, you may not be able to appreciate it. This is especially true if you were neglected or emotionally abused as a child. You may have a tendency to look for the slightest flaw and focus on your imperfections so much they seem to overshadow all your other good qualities. Some people take this to such an extreme that they develop a disorder called body dysmorphic disorder, or BDD.

Many teens worry incessantly about their weight and appearance, but some become obsessed with a specific flaw or perceived defect. This was the case with Kimberly, age sixteen. Kimberly was convinced that her chin is too big. She constantly looked in the mirror, examining her chin from various angles, and she obsessed about which hairstyle would best camouflage it. When others tried to tell her that her chin looked fine, she didn't believe them. In fact, she pressured her parents into sending her to a plastic surgeon to correct the problem. When her parents refused to allow her to get the surgery, she became very upset and refused to go to school anymore. Her behavior signaled to her parents—rightly so—that this was more than the typical teen obsession with looks. Kimberly needed therapy.

Obsessors and Avoiders

People who have issues with self-esteem, body image, and self-criticism tend to fall into two major categories—obsessors and avoiders—and they tend to deal with the mirror in very different ways.

Obsessors are preoccupied with the way they look and tend to look in the mirror often, if not constantly. They scrutinize their facial features, their hair, and their complexion, and they obsess about any body part that they feel is too fat, too thin, too long or short, or too crooked. When they are getting dressed, they obsess over whether a garment looks good on them, and throughout the day they check the mirror often to see if they appear okay.

Avoiders may check the mirror briefly as they get dressed or occasionally throughout the day to make sure their hair or makeup is okay, but otherwise they seldom look in the mirror. Many avoiders look in the mirror without really looking—just a quick glance to make sure their clothes match or their lipstick isn't smeared—but they avoid looking too closely. This avoidance of the mirror may be caused by a basic disapproval of their looks. For this reason it is painful for them to look at themselves. Others feel so ugly on the inside that they see only ugliness when they look in the mirror—no matter how attractive they actually are.

How Is Our Body Image Created?

To a great extent, our body image comes from the physical and emotional input we received as children. Although media-driven images and expectations certainly have an effect, messages from significant others have an even more dramatic impact on how we feel physically and emotionally about our bodies as adults.

Parents have the most profound effect on our body image. If they like how we look and tell us so, we face the world with a head start. If, on the other hand, our parents dislike our appearance, our body image will be influenced in a negative way.

Carlos began to dislike his body when he was quite young. This is how he explained it to me: "My dad was a jock and he wanted me to be one, too. But I was more frail, like my mother. He was constantly on me to gain weight and to 'toughen up,' but no matter how much I ate or exercised I was still too thin. I knew my dad was disappointed in how I looked, and it bothered me a lot and made me self-conscious.

When I was in school I hated gym class and never wanted to take off my shirt because I was ashamed of my underdeveloped chest."

When parents place a great deal of importance on physical appearance, they often instill in their children a tendency to overemphasize looks. This was the case with Annette: "My mother was very pretty and spent a lot of time on her appearance. She taught me to do the same, starting when I was very young. If I had one hair out of place, she got on me. My dad also seemed to pay a lot of attention to how my mom and I looked. He was always making comments about how beautiful my mom was, and he always told me that I looked cute. But I knew I'd never be as beautiful as my mother because I didn't inherit her good looks. I grew up thinking that beauty was the most important thing a woman had to offer a man and that in order to keep a man you have to work on looking good all the time."

Another factor that influences your body image is whether your parents are satisfied with the way *they* look. Parents with a poor body image can pass on their negative attitudes and feelings to their children, causing them to dislike their own bodies. This is especially true if you resemble a parent who dislikes his or her body.

Madeline's mother, who was of Armenian descent, had a great deal of body hair—as did everyone on her mother's side of the family. She had dark hair on her arms, thighs, and calves, and even on her face. "When I was little I remember my mother using a product called Nair to remove hair from different parts of her body. She was always worried about hair growing back," Madeline shared with me. "When I was around twelve and I started to develop she began worrying about my body hair. She taught me how to use the depilatory and nagged at me to use it as soon as even the slightest bit of hair started coming back. I hated using it. It stank and it made a mess. And sometimes it gave me a rash. But she insisted I use it even when I protested. When I became an adolescent I began to feel self-conscious about being so hairy and I became as obsessed as my mother about always making sure it was removed. I noticed that other girls weren't as hairy as I was and somehow it became a source of shame for me. I began to hate my body for being so hairy."

Shelly's mother also projected her own poor body image onto her daughter. "From the time I was a little girl I remember my mother was always battling with her weight. She went on all kinds of crash diets, sometimes starving herself for days. When I reached ten years old, she started focusing on my weight as well. The doctor told her I was of normal weight and I would probably grow out of my baby fat, but she didn't believe him. She started me on diets and paying a lot of attention to what I ate."

This continued throughout junior high school. By the time Shelly entered high school, she had a serious problem with her self-image. She thought she was fat even though she wasn't. "I even saw myself as overweight when I looked in the mirror, although I was actually getting thinner and thinner." By the time Shelly reached sixteen, she was throwing up any food she ate and had become anorexic. I have worked with Shelly for the past two years, helping her overcome her problem and to see herself accurately instead of so critically.

Like Shelly, many people have negative body images, not because they have unattractive bodies but because they see themselves inaccurately. Their images of their physical selves are distorted, either because they see their overall size and shape as much fatter, thinner, taller or shorter than they actually are, or because they view specific body parts in a distorted way. When the latter occurs, not only do they perceive their long nose, acne, wide hips, sagging breasts, or large butts as more grotesque than they are, but they see these imagined or real flaws as dominating their entire physical selves, as Carla did: "Everyone tells me that I am so pretty, but I know I'm really not. They don't know I have these huge hips and thighs because I do such a good job of hiding them. But when I look in the mirror all I see are my hips and thighs. They disgust me so much that I refuse to wear a bathing suit or shorts. I know other people would be just as disgusted if they ever saw how I really look." Unfortunately, Carla has been blinded to her other physical attributes—her beautiful skin and hair, her lovely shoulders and breasts, her striking facial features.

Carla is not alone. Many people are poor judges of themselves and have a distorted view of how they impress others. Most people, especially women, are not as unattractive as they think they are. Recent research has found that only 2 percent of women are satisfied with the way they look. Studies have shown that relatively few women look in the mirror without focusing on all the things they'd like to change, whereas men tend to be more accepting of what they see. Women tend to distort their perceptions of their bodies negatively, while men—just as unrealistically—distort their perceptions in a positive, self-aggrandizing way.

Women put an overemphasis on the way their bodies look and assume that men are attracted to them solely or primarily because of their bodies. Although our culture does in fact place a high value on physical attractiveness, women don't take into account their personalities, their wits, their minds, their sensitivity, their ability to relate to others, and most important, their ability to love.

Do You Judge Yourself Accurately?

Most people's poor body image reflects the fact that something occurred in childhood to erode their confidence. Unfortunately, we are all taught from an early age that attractive people are also more worthy (for example, recent research shows that parents treat their attractive children better than their unattractive children). And we are all taught just what *is* considered attractive in our particular social circle. This training begins very early on, when the cutest babies and toddlers are given the most attention by outsiders. Slowly, as children grow up, they will be treated a certain way depending on how cute they are, what kind of clothes they wear, and what color skin they have.

It should be no surprise that studies have shown that attractive children tend to develop more self-confidence and have higher self-esteem than children who are perceived as less attractive. If adults smiled approvingly and told you how cute or how pretty or how handsome you were as you were growing up, you probably felt very good about your body and the way you looked. On the other hand, if insensitive adults said things such as, "My, she is a fat one, isn't she?" or "He must look like his father" (implying that he doesn't look like his *attractive* mother), you probably ended up not feeling very good about your appearance.

Peer Acceptance and Rejection

It is very important to children and adolescents that they be accepted by their peers. If they have this acceptance, they tend to have high self-esteem, while those who experience rejection, teasing, or indifference tend to have lower self-esteem. Name-calling is particularly hurtful to children and can affect their body image negatively. Names such as "Fatso" can stay with a person for a lifetime, as happened to Hank: "It's pretty difficult to think of yourself as sexually attractive to women when you were called a "nerd" or a "fag" most of your childhood. Those words still ring in my ears every time I even think of asking a girl out."

Rejection or indifference from the opposite sex can be particularly devastating to a person's body image and can be the start of an adolescent believing that she or he is not attractive or desirable, as it did with Ellen: "Boys just never paid any attention to me in school. I was taller than most of them and my parents couldn't afford to buy my clothes at a specialty store, so they were usually either too short or too long. By the time I was in junior high school I just gave up trying to get their attention."

The Effects of Emotional Abuse, Neglect, and Smothering on Our Body Image

We all have issues with our bodies. We feel we are too fat or too short or that our bodies are not in proportion. But if we were emotionally abused or deprived in childhood we tend to have far greater body issues. We may have taken on our parents' negative messages and projections about our bodies in comments like "God help you, you've got the Hanson nose." But more important, when we look in the mirror we often see our own self-loathing reflected back on ourselves—the self-loathing that often comes from having been criticized, ignored, or viewed with contempt by our parents.

If a child is emotionally, physically, or sexually abused, she or he is especially likely to have a problematic body image. Nothing erodes a child's confidence more than experiencing this kind of abuse, particularly when it comes from parents. This is partly because children tend to blame themselves instead of being willing to experience the alienation that feeling anger toward the abusive parent can create. A great deal of this self-blame turns into self-loathing—in particular a hatred of the child's own body.

Many emotionally abusive parents attack their child's physical appearance, as in the case of Brenda: "My father would periodically go on a rampage—shouting and throwing things at my mother and then bursting into my bedroom and yelling horrible things at me. He'd tell me that I was ugly and that no man would ever want me. I can't tell you how many times I've heard the same words over and over in my own head."

Fathers have a tremendous effect on a daughter's body image. If a girl knows that her father loves her and thinks she is attractive, she is more likely to feel attractive to other men. If, on the other hand, she feels rejected by her father or thinks he sees her as unattractive, she will generalize this to all men.

When the body is labeled inadequate, especially by a parent, the self feels diminished as well. This can lead to self-defeating behaviors. Adults who were abused as children often ignore, neglect, and even abuse their bodies, seeing them as objects of shame. Survivors of abuse tend to cover up their bodies, hiding them from themselves and the rest of the world.

Parental neglect, contempt, or verbal abuse can convince a child that she is completely worthless, unlovable, and ugly inside and out. This was the case with my client Marilyn: "I can't look in a mirror. I hate what I see there. I only look in the mirror for a few seconds to comb my hair or put on some lipstick." The reason Marilyn felt this way toward herself was that both her parents treated her with contempt. They made it clear that they did not want her and that she was in the way. Parental criticism and contempt can cause children to hate themselves and their bodies, often leading to self-mutilation and other self-destructive behaviors. In order to heal this self-hatred, Marilyn needed to work on rejecting the negative parental messages that helped to create it. (You will learn how to do this in part two of this book.)

EXERCISE: WHAT WERE THE MESSAGES YOU RECEIVED?

1. Make a list of all the messages concerning your body that you remember receiving from peers, siblings, and friends from the time when you were a child until the present. Include nicknames and insults from your siblings and peers, and things that you have been told by friends and lovers.

2. List the messages you received from your parents concerning your body. Include verbal and nonverbal messages.

3. Review your two lists and put a star beside each message that still has an effect on you (the ones you still believe, and the ones that are still replayed in your head).

Children who are highly criticized by their parents, especially when their bodies are criticized, tend to internalize the quest for flaws. They look at their bodies in a similarly critical way, evaluating and rejecting the slightest imperfections. As long as we constantly compare ourselves to an ideal standard, we conclude that self-improvement is necessary for self-acceptance.

The following exercise was designed to help you begin to view your body in an entirely different way.

EXERCISE: WHAT IS YOUR BODY TRYING TO TELL YOU?

1. Look at your face in the mirror. What does your face tell you about yourself? For example, do you look sad? Angry? Afraid? Ashamed?

2. Come closer to the mirror. Look deep into your eyes. What do you see there? Fear? Anger? Sadness? Shame?

3. In a full-length mirror take a close look at your body, not from the standpoint of evaluating it but from the perspective of seeing what your body says about you. What is your body telling you about yourself? Is it trying to tell you that you are angry? Sad? Afraid? Ashamed? Is it trying to tell you that you are not taking care of it properly—that you are neglecting it the same way your parents did? Is it trying to tell you that you are abusing it the same way your parents

did? Is your body telling you that it is trying to protect you from further harm?

4. Take a close look at your posture. Do you stand up straight or do you tend to hunch over? Is one shoulder higher than the other? What do you think these things say about you?

Body Issues as Red Flags

Sometimes the parts of our bodies we dislike the most are caused by genetics—we inherit a parent's nose or a predisposition to be overly thin. But other times a problem body area is a red flag, telling us that something is wrong. For example, obese people often use eating to deny inner pain. Allowing themselves to acknowledge and feel their pain can help to alleviate the need to suppress feelings with food.

Our bodies are mirrors. They reflect what is really going on inside of us. If you are sad, your face and your body will reflect this sadness in some way. If you look deep into your eyes, you will see the sadness and the pain that is inside you. If you look at your expression, you will likely see sadness in the downturn of your mouth, stress in the pinched lines between your brows.

Our body also reflects how we really feel about ourselves. If we are filled with self-loathing, we will likely see it in our bodies. It might be revealed by being far too thin from depriving ourselves of needed nourishment. It may be revealed by punishing our bodies with alcohol or drugs. Or it may be revealed by the scarring on our arms from continual cutting.

When Anna was very young, her parents didn't expect anything good or bad from her. They just didn't see her. "It was like I didn't register to them. They were so busy with their own lives, so focused on their own feelings and needs, that they couldn't pay attention to mine." So Anna did to herself what her parents did to her—she rendered herself invisible. She isolated herself in her room and got lost in books. She denied her feelings and hid from her true self.

Then, when Anna became older, her parents often punished her for things she didn't do. When she tried to defend herself, they became even more angry and rejecting.

"I was so used to not being seen that when they started accusing me of things I hadn't done it felt horribly painful. I tried to become a turtle, going inside an imaginary shell so I'd be out of reach of their accusatory comments. And I hid from my pain by eating. I had no other way to comfort or soothe myself. I'd tell myself, 'It doesn't matter what I do,' and 'It doesn't do any good to defend myself or to get angry,' and so I'd sneak food into my room and stuff my feelings down. I turned all my anger onto myself."

At school Anna was deeply afraid of further rejection, so she kept to herself. "I had perfected my turtle act by the time I was in the third grade. No one seemed to notice me and that's exactly the way I wanted it. On the inside, of course, I was starving for love, but on the outside I created a hard shell that kept everybody away.

As Anna told her story, I was struck by how, in some ways, she actually did look like a turtle. She had short arms and legs and her trunk had a boxy look to it—the way a turtle would look if it stood on its hind legs. She seemed to have almost no neck at all. And there was an invisible quality to Anna. She tended to wear very muted colors, and nothing about her features really stood out. I had once seen her at a café near my office. She said hello to me, but I did not recognize her. It wasn't until she mentioned seeing me at our next session that I realized that she was the woman who had said hello.

As it turned out, Anna had not only made her body nearly invisible but she had also created an emotional mask to protect her as well. "No one really knows me. I won't let them see behind my mask. I'm afraid of what will happen if I show people who I really am."

Your body also acts as a protector of your emotions and your very self. Marianne's mother constantly criticized her from the time she was a very small child, especially about the way she looked. First she was too thin, and so her mother gave her cod liver oil, shots, and vitamins to fatten her up. Then she became too fat and was put on an endless series of diets. When she didn't grow tall enough to offset her weight, her mother took her to the doctor to see if her growth was stunted in some way. When she finally did start gaining height, her mother ridiculed her and told her no man would want her because she would be taller than he was. By the time Marianne reached adolescence, she determined that she could never satisfy her mother and that she had to hide herself from her mother's critical eye. She did this by gaining an enormous amount of weight.

Although it may have seemed self-defeating to gain weight and thus invite her mother's criticism, in reality Marianne was simply trying to defend herself against her mother's constant scrutiny. As long as her mother was distracted by her weight, she didn't delve into deeper aspects of Marianne's personality. Her weight acted as a defensive wall, protecting her from her mother's scrutinizing gaze. And by staying overweight she didn't pose a threat to her mother's fragile ego— she was no competition. Finally, she stayed fat because it kept her from displeasing her mother by having an independent life. Boys didn't ask her out and so her mother could keep her tied to her emotionally.

Reconnecting with Your Body

Much of the damage caused by emotional abuse, neglect, and smothering shows up in a disconnection with the body and in distortions of body image. This can lead to eating disorders such as compulsive overeating, bulimia, and anorexia. Children who were emotionally abused or deprived are often out of touch with their bodies and do not know how to read their body's sensations and messages. The pain of rejection, humiliation, or deprivation may have been so intense that they had to numb themselves against it. If no one was there to comfort them when they were in discomfort or pain, they had to turn off the sensation or emotion. One of the main problems that these people have is an inability to soothe themselves, because this ability is typically learned from experiencing the soothing efforts of a parent.

Emotionally abusive parents do not respond appropriately to their child's emotions and/or body sensations. They tend to be out of touch with their child's emotions and to interpet and respond to them according to their own biases, moods, needs, and past experiences. For example, if a parent was laughed at when she cried, she will tend to do the same to her own child. Emotionally abusive or depriving parents also tend to mislabel their child's feelings and needs, often telling her she is not really feeling what she is feeling (for example, if a parent was too busy to stop to feed his child, he tells the child he is not really hungry). Because the body gives us vital clues as to what is going on with us emotionally, the inability to understand our body's messages keeps us from having a deep understanding of ourselves. If we can't understand our bodily sensations, who are we? Certainly we are more than our thoughts.

People who were emotionally abused or deprived can also suffer from body-image distortions. Some feel smaller while others feel bigger than they actually are. Many feel they are far less attractive than they really are due to negative parental messages in the form of criticism, judgments, and shaming.

My client Linda is an exceptionally beautiful woman with a mane of curly black hair, large brown eyes, and a beautiful, athletic body. But she feels she is very plain and that men find her ordinary, because her father constantly criticized the way she looked when she was growing up. "My dad didn't like the fact that I resembled my mother and not his side of the family, who had straight blonde hair and blue eyes. He wanted me to be sexy and curvy, but I was always too skinny. He teased me mercilessly about how much I looked like a little boy."

In order to heal the damage caused by emotional abuse and neglect, you will need to learn how to rediscover yourself through your emotions and physical sensations, and to reconnect with your body. Throughout this book I present creative techniques to facilitate this reconnection, such as writing exercises, creating self-portraits, and expressing your emotions through art. But it will be through mirror work that the real changes will take place. By utilizing the concept of the "body as mirror" and by doing various exercises actually using the mirror, you will be able to heal your distorted body image and begin to see yourself in a more realistic and positive way.

We are all fascinated and repelled by our own image in the mirror. Most of us are preoccupied with our body image, how we look to others, and how to make ourselves more attractive. But it is important to understand that unless we heal ourselves on the inside, we will not like the person we see in the mirror. The idea that you can actually use the mirror to help heal your inner wounds may sound intriguing to you.

On the other hand, it may turn you off or frighten you. If this is your situation, try the various mirror exercises one time to see if they can be effective for you.

Mirror Therapy Assignment #3: Mirror, Mirror, on the Wall

1. Stand close to your bathroom mirror and look at your face. Do you generally have a positive or a negative impression of how your face looks? If you have a negative impression, write down the reasons why you don't like your face.

2. Closely examine each of your features, one by one. As you look at each feature, ask yourself the following questions: "Do I like this feature?" "What is it about this feature that I like or dislike?" "Does this feature remind me of anyone in my family?"

3. Make a list of messages you feel you were given by your parents (or other significant caretakers) about your face. The messages may have been spoken out loud or they may have been given to you nonverbally (with negative looks or the absence of praise).

4. Now look at your body in a full-length mirror. Start by asking yourself if you like or dislike how your body looks. Then try to remember any messages you may have received about your body from your parents.

5. As you did with your face, look at each part of your body (your arms, your chest, your stomach) and ask yourself, "Do I like this part of my body?" "What is it about this part of my body that I like or dislike?" "Does this part of my body remind me of anyone else in my family?"

6. You may have felt anxious or embarrassed as you did this exercise. Write down any feelings that arose inside you. Don't judge or analyze the feelings; just describe them.

4

How Mirror Therapy Works

Mirror, mirror, on the wall, who's the fairest of them all?

MIRROR THERAPY IS NOT BASED on one particular technique. Instead, it centers on a series of psychological truths and two major processes I call "Shattering Your Parental Mirror" (rejecting the distorted images you received from your emotionally abusive or neglectful parents) and "Creating a New Mirror" (replacing the distorted images with a more accurate reflection of who you really are). These two major processes include a series of exercises and homework assignments, some involving an actual mirror.

The Basic Premises of Mirror Therapy

Mirror Therapy is based on the following psychological truths:

1. Problems with low self-esteem and poor body image are often caused by negative parental messages communicated through emotional abuse, neglect, or smothering.

2. The only real alternative to self-criticism is knowing the truth about who you are. If you have a deep belief that you are worthless, you must discover where that belief came from and why you believe it is true.

3. People with a history of abuse or neglect tend to remain enmeshed with their parents out of a desperate desire to get what they did not get as children.

4. Parental emotional abuse creates a negative internal judge or pathological inner critic.

5. Survivors of emotional abuse or neglect often do not develop a clear and undistorted image of themselves. By keeping a Mirror Journal, creating a word self-portrait, and completing various other activities, survivors can gain a clearer image of themselves—their likes and dislikes, and their values, goals, and dreams.

6. Parents project their own unresolved issues onto their children. In order to heal from the damage this causes, adult children need to reject the distorted mirror their parents put on them and create a new mirror that reflects more accurately who they actually are.

7. People who were emotionally abused or neglected in childhood tend to be numb to their emotions, feel sideswiped by them, or feel overwhelmed when their emotions build up.

8. Starting in infancy, children need positive, empathetic mirroring from their parents in order to know that they have worth. When a child is treated with empathy, that is, when parents sensitively respond to the child's thoughts and feelings, the child learns that she is worthy of love and is worthwhile. Her empathy and compassion for herself grow as she mirrors inside what the outside world has revealed to her about her self-worth. If, on the other hand, a child is not given this empathetic mirroring, she doesn't feel loved and is not able to feel compassionate toward herself.

9. Adults who were emotionally abused or deprived need to create a nurturing, responsive, internal "mother" and a safe, powerful, internal "father" in order to provide for themselves what they missed out on as a child. This involves learning nurturing skills and how to set effective limits.

10. If a child's needs and feelings are continually ignored or discounted, he will not know how to soothe himself.

11. By committing to the process of change and growth, we can discover that when we are more accepting of ourselves—even with all our faults and flaws—we are free to become the person we were meant to be.

12. People who were emotionally abused or neglected tend to be disconnected from their emotions and their bodies. Through body image exercises and feelings exercises, survivors can reconnect with these important aspects of themselves.

13. Children mirror what they see in life, especially what their parents do. Parents who behave in inappropriate ways become unhealthy role models for their children.

Throughout the rest of this book, beginning with chapter 5, I will remind you of these premises in the form of "psychological truths" at the end of each chapter. Each psychological truth will correspond to the focus of each chapter and will serve as a suggestion for contemplation and a basic review.

Mirror Therapy is also based on the following ideas: If you have low self-esteem and a poor body image and/or tend to be self-critical, the image you see in the mirror often reflects how your parents and other primary caretakers perceived you. Negative parenting experiences often cause us to see ourselves through a distorted lens. When parents are inattentive, angry, or self-absorbed, the mirror they hold up for their children reflects a distorted vision of reality. When they are overly critical, shaming, or verbally abusive, children see a distorted and unrealistic image of themselves. It is like looking at yourself in a fun-house hall of mirrors—you can't really see yourself accurately because the mirror itself is distorted. Unfortunately, children have no way of knowing that the image they see is distorted, and so they come to believe that the reflection is real.

Mirror Therapy can help you provide for yourself your own positive mirroring experiences and reject the negative messages and projections put on you by your parents. It will also help you heal from your parents' lack of proper mirroring. By giving back the negative projections your parents placed upon you and then providing for yourself the positive empathetic mirroring you did not receive as a child, you can rid yourself of your distorted, negative self-image. This will be done with a series of exercises and practices specifically developed to overcome neglect, shame, negative parental messages, and inadequate role modeling.

The Mirror Therapy process will also help you to understand the concept of the judge (or superego or inner critic) and will teach you how to overcome its negative influence in your life as well as self-soothing techniques and how to have compassion for yourself.

Mirroring and Projection

Mirroring is a word used to describe the empathetic responsiveness many parents have toward their child's needs, activities, and wishes. Mirroring teaches the child which of his potential qualities are most highly esteemed and valued. Mirroring also validates the child as to who he is and affirms his worth.

Projection is an unconscious defense mechanism. What is emotionally unacceptable to the self is unconsciously rejected and attributed to others. Many parents emotionally abuse, neglect, or smother their children by neglecting to practice proper mirroring or by projecting their own unacceptable, rejected qualities onto them.

Mirroring and projection play an important role in creating our self-image. For example, most parents feel a rush of emotion when they first see their newborn infant. They have an overwhelming feeling of love and a deep desire to nurture their baby and protect it from harm. Unfortunately, some parents do not feel this rush of love, nor do they feel a strong nurturing or protective instinct. Some feel nothing. Others are overwhelmed with fear.

Parents who feel love for their infants also love to look at their baby. They marvel at every little thing the child does; every gesture or facial expression is endearing to them and they naturally smile at the child in adoration. These adoring, approving looks are like a magic potion to a baby, imbuing him with confidence and a strong sense of self.

Parents who do not feel love for their infant may do everything necessary to take care of their child properly and yet they will not naturally mirror (repeat or mimic) their infant's facial gestures or shower their infant with unconditional love. While they may hold their infant closely and give him the necessary nutrition, they may look away or become preoccupied with something else. As a result, the infant does not receive the adoring attention or empathetic mirroring he needs.

Parents who were themselves neglected or abused in childhood tend to treat their own children the way they were treated. For example, if a mother did not receive empathetic mirroring from her own mother, she will probably not know how to give it to her baby. If a father was overly criticized or shamed by his parents, he will likely project his bad feelings about himself onto his own children and end up treating them in the same ways he was treated.

During the stages of development from about two to four years of age (known as the rapprochement phase), a child builds on what he has already learned. This involves the child's increasing discovery that he is a separate, autonomous self. During this phase the child constantly references back and forth, from himself to his parent or caretaker, in order to validate that it is all right to move out on his own. You have no doubt noticed this when watching toddlers. They reach out to touch something and then look back at their parent for his or her reaction.

A child checks the facial expressions, body language, and tone of voice of people around her—particularly her parents—to determine what kind of person she is. The ones close to her become reflections of her self—her mirrors. If these mirrors are smiling, the child feels good about herself; if they are frowning, she may become frightened and not feel so good about herself. As Nancy Napier, the author of *Recreating Your Self*, stated: "The mirrors in a child's life convey a wide variety of messages about the self. They may say she is worthwhile or lovable, or that she is a nuisance or unlovable."

According to Napier, these reflections create a powerful foundation for the child's internal sense of self. If parents are consistently remote, irritated, or hostile, the messages coming to the child will be self-diminishing and may create in a child a certain lack of acceptance of himself, because, as children, we believe what people reflect to us. As children, we have neither the cognitive nor the emotional ability to understand that Mother had a hard day and would snap at *anyone* she had to deal with. Instead, we conclude that we are the cause of our mother's response, which in turn can become the belief that we are bad, that there is something wrong with us, or that we do not deserve to be treated well.

Parents are not the only ones who reflect self-diminishing beliefs back to us. Children also see mirrors in other family members, other caretakers, teachers, friends, and authority figures. The responses of all these people are taken in as reflections of the developing self. When these reflections are similar to the negative reflections from parents, children believe even more certainly that they are bad, they are to blame, or they are unlovable. Conversely, when the reflections from those mirrors are consistently positive, good feelings about the self are enhanced and reinforced. Unfortunately, many who grow up in abusive or neglectful homes tend to receive more self-diminishing than self-enhancing reflections.

How to Use This Book

As you read on, I encourage you to keep a Mirror Journal to record your feelings, reactions, and progress. You may wish to use your Mirror Journal for the many exercises in these chapters as well as for the various letters I encourage you to write throughout the book.

I suggest you attempt to read only one chapter per week, especially as you get into the actual Mirror Therapy program (parts two and three). It is best to take in the information slowly. Each chapter has many exercises for you to complete. At the end of each chapter you will find a "homework assignment" for the week. I encourage you to do the exercises and these assignments because they are an important aspect of the healing process. Readers of my previous books have consistently given me feedback that they experienced more progress when they did the exercises.

The Mirror Therapy program presented in this book is considered an adjunct to professional therapy, especially if you were emotionally abused as a child. Although you can do the exercises on your own and can gain a better understanding of why you are the way you are from reading the book, a professional therapist can help you with some of the deeper issues, such as healing abandonment wounds and shame. The consistent, positive regard you receive from a good therapist (positive mirroring) can help heal the wounds caused by overly critical or overly shaming parents. This sense of approval from an authority figure has the potential to be enormously healing.

Mirror Therapy techniques are also intended to be tools for psychotherapists working with people with low self-esteem, powerful inner critics, and deep shame issues. I offer a combination of cognitive restructuring techniques that are best used in cases of *situational* low self-esteem (someone whose low self-esteem tends to come up only in specific areas such as work or sexual performance), while they have confidence in other aspects of their lives. Low self-esteem that is *characterological*, on the other hand, usually has roots in early experiences of abuse or abandonment. The sense of "badness" or "wrongness" is more global and tends to affect many areas of their lives. In this case, changing a client's thoughts is not enough. The main therapeutic focus needs to be on helping the client to re-create her identity and in some ways start over, since it is her negative identity that gives rise to her negative thoughts. Helping clients begin to give to themselves what they missed out on in childhood (positive mirroring, a nurturing, responsive, internal mother, and a safe, powerful, internal father to help them set limits) will help them to "grow themselves up" in a healthy way. Encouraging them to become more compassionate toward themselves will help them quiet their inner critics and overcome their shame.

MIRROR THERAPY ASSIGNMENT #4

List the ways you feel your parents projected their own problems or unmet needs onto you.

PART TWO

Shattering Your Distorted Parental Mirror

5

Rejecting Your Parents' Negative Reflection

There is nothing wrong with you. Anyone who says something is wrong is wrong.

—RENAIS JEANNE HILL

We must never allow other people's limited perceptions to define us.

—VIRGINIA SATIR

WE DO NOT NEED AN ACTUAL MIRROR to see our reflections. We can see them in the way we treat ourselves, the way others perceive us and treat us, and in the ways our lives reflect how we feel about ourselves. Once you have become aware of the distorted image you have of yourself, you can begin to reject the inaccurate mirror your parents provided and replace it with a more accurate reflection.

Shattering Your Distorted Image

Before you can create a new, healthy image of yourself, you first need to shatter the distorted image placed on you through your parents' actions and beliefs. This includes:

1. Facing the truth and releasing pent-up emotions concerning the abuse or neglect you experienced

2. Placing responsibility where it belongs and giving back your parents' projections

3. Turning your shame into righteous anger

4. Identifying and countering negative beliefs

Face the Truth and Express Pent-Up Emotions

Earlier, you may have experienced strong emotions as you read about what constitutes childhood emotional abuse and neglect and the effects they can have on a child's sense of self and self-esteem. It can be quite painful to admit that you were abused or neglected in these ways and that you likely suffered from some or all of these effects. You may experience tremendous pain as you remember how it felt to be treated the way you were, and you may become extremely angry at the ones who abused or neglected you. You may feel a deep sense of loss as your idealized picture of your childhood or your positive image of a parent or another family member or adored caregiver is tarnished forever.

When we finally do face the truth about what happened to us as children, we can become overwhelmed with grief, sadness, and anger. Allow yourself to feel these emotions. Don't try to fight them off; you've probably been doing that for too long. Allow your emotions to flow out of you. Cry for the little child who was mistreated in such terrible ways. Get angry at how the little child you once were was used or abused by adults who should have known better—adults who were supposed to protect you.

In order to shatter your negative parental mirror and raise your self-esteem, you must revisit the original wounding. Unfortunately, most people who were neglected or abused box off their pain and try to put it out of their minds. But this never really works. Experiences of neglect and emotional abuse continue to wear you down emotionally, insidiously whittling away at your self-esteem.

Many people who were neglected or abused stay stuck in anger or pain and never move through their feelings. Instead, they turn their feelings of anger on themselves and become depressed or riddled with unnecessary (and unhealthy) guilt and shame. Some punish themselves by being self-destructive—smoking, driving too fast, or provoking a fight with someone. Others numb themselves to their feelings and are unable to access their anger and pain from the past.

Emotions that go unexpressed often lie dormant inside us until someone or something reminds us of our past and triggers a memory—and the feeling. When this happens we can become depressed and self-critical or lash out at the ones closest to us when our real target is someone from the past—someone we were likely afraid to express our emotions to at the time.

It can be frightening to lift the veil of denial—our tendency to ignore, suppress, or repress painful realities, thoughts, and feelings. The scariest part is experiencing the intense feelings that lurk just below denial's surface. You may need professional help in dealing with all these strong emotions. For now, allow yourself to experience whatever it is that you are feeling and remember the following:

- Even though it may feel as if it is happening in the present, it will help if you remind yourself that what you are feeling are memories of the emotions you experienced as a child. These things are not happening to you in the present. You have already survived your childhood and the painful things that happened to you.

- It helps if you breathe into an emotion. As it is with physical pain, breathing into the feeling tends to decrease it and makes it less overwhelming.

- As powerful and overwhelming as emotions can be, they are actually positive forces intended to help you process an experience.

- As long as you don't allow yourself to become overwhelmed by your emotions, they will help you come out of and stay out of denial.

- Allowing yourself to feel and express your hidden emotions from the past will help heal your wounds from the past.

Exercise: Your Feelings about the Abuse

1. Earlier you made a list of all the ways you were neglected or abused as a child. Return to your list and for each item write about the following:

   - How you felt at the time
   - The effect the neglect or abuse had on you at the time
   - How you feel now as you remember the experience
   - What effect you believe the experience has had on you long term

   As you write about each incident of neglect or abuse, allow yourself to feel whatever emotions come up for you. It is appropriate for you to feel angry, enraged, afraid, terrified, sad, grief-stricken, guilty, ashamed, or any other emotions you may feel. On the other hand, do not become alarmed if you do not feel anything. Survivors of childhood abuse and neglect often numb themselves to their feelings as a self-protective mechanism.

2. If at all possible, share your writings with at least one other person. Most victims of childhood neglect or abuse did not have what is called a compassionate witness to their pain and anguish. Telling a loved one about what happened to you and receiving your loved one's support and kindness can be a major step in the healing process. For example, experts such as Alice Miller have found that a sympathetic and understanding witness to a child's suffering is a crucial prerequisite to empathy in adulthood. Without empathy, we cannot be sensitive to the pain of others.

Now that you know the truth, the truth is yours to use for recovery. You have a better idea of what physical and emotional pain you endured and what long-term effects you are suffering from. There is healing in discovering the truth, facing it, and, finally, accepting it. Your realization of the facts about your own neglect and abuse clears the way for dealing with your anger and resolving your relationships with your family. You have lived with lies, secrecy, and deception for a long time, and it has been painful. Learning to live with the truth will help free you from the pain and lead you toward a fuller, richer life.

Place Responsibility Where It Belongs and Give Back Your Parents' Projections

You met Stephen earlier (home was a cold place where his mother didn't like him). When Stephen and I started working together, I asked him how he felt about the way his parents had treated him. Even though he wasn't close to either of them, he didn't seem to have any strong feelings about them one way or the other. "I haven't seen my mother in years, and then it is only at family gatherings, where I manage to greet her politely. I don't want anything to do with her. My father and I have a surface relationship. We talk on the phone about twice a month but we don't really say anything of consequence."

After several months of working together, Stephen began to get more in touch with some of his anger toward his parents. But this didn't sit well with him. "I'm responsible for the good and bad about me—not my parents. I pretty much raised myself. It's difficult for me to admit that I'm at the effect of anybody, much less them."

Many people who were neglected or emotionally abused feel the same way Stephen does. They prefer to take responsibility for their lives rather than "blame" their parents. But holding your parents responsible for the way they neglected or abused you and the effects this kind of treatment had on your self-esteem is not the same as blaming them. Blaming keeps us stuck in the problem, whereas righteous anger helps us move through the problem. People who refuse to get angry at their parents tend to sink into self-blame, shame, and depression. It is much healthier to allow yourself your righteous anger than to turn that anger on yourself. By getting angry at your parents for their negative treatment, you are also more likely to be able to reject the negative messages that came along with that treatment— negative messages that still influence you today.

Earlier we discussed the concept of projection. It is very possible that the negative messages, criticism, and abusive treatment you received from your parents were a result of your parents' projecting onto you aspects of themselves they disapprove of or deny. If this is the case, it is important that you give back these projections. For example, Dustin's mother constantly told him as he was growing up that he was lazy and spoiled. She complained about his not cleaning up his room, and whenever he asked for money for school supplies or other necessities, she accused him of being greedy and ungrateful. With a little reality check gleaned from therapy and from learning more about his mother's history, Dustin discovered that he wasn't lazy at all and he certainly wasn't spoiled. In fact, he spent most of his childhood and adolescence being depressed and feeling guilty for bothering his mother about money. As it turns out, Dustin's mother had been accused of the same things when she was growing up and she was more than likely depressed as well.

Give Back Your Parents' Shame

As mentioned earlier, many survivors of emotional abuse and neglect feel a lot of shame about themselves and their bodies. The inner experience of shame is to feel seen or perceived by others in a painfully diminished way. The self feels exposed and it is this sudden, unexpected feeling of exposure and accompanying self-consciousness that characterizes the essential nature of shame. Shame also causes an overwhelming belief that one is fundamentally deficient in some vital way as a human being. To live with shame is to feel alienated and defeated. It is to believe you are never quite good enough.

As Jane Middelton-Moz explained in *Shame and Guilt*, "Debilitating shame is an isolating experience that makes us think we are completely alone and unique in our unlovability. It is a feeling that we are intensely and profoundly unlovable. Debilitating shame is a state of self-hate and self-devaluation that is comparable to little else. It makes us feel that life is happening to us and that we are helpless in the wake of that happening."

Although you may *intellectually* understand that the abuse or neglect was not your fault, you may not know it *emotionally*. You may still blame yourself. Absolutely nothing you did as a child warranted any kind of neglect or emotional, physical, or sexual abuse that you experienced. You did not cry so much that your mother had to finally ignore your cries and leave you all alone in your crib for hours at a time. You were not such a demanding child that your parents had to ignore you. You didn't have such an inflated ego that your father had to "bring you down a notch or two" by telling you that you were stupid. Your parents' (or other abusers') reactions were their responsibility and theirs alone. It is vital that you understand this.

Turn Your Shame into Righteous Anger

Even if you did not have a shaming parent, if you were emotionally abused or neglected, you no doubt suffered from heavy doses of shame. This shame needs to be turned into anger in order for you to shatter the mirror that shaming creates.

Anger pushes away shame. Releasing your anger toward your abusers will help you stop blaming yourself. Getting angry at your abuser will affirm your innocence, and the vital force of anger will be moving in the right direction: outward instead of inward.

EXERCISE: GIVE THE SHAME BACK TO YOUR ABUSER

1. Sit comfortably and breathe deeply.
2. Imagine you are looking inside your body. Find any shame or bad feelings you might have there.
3. Imagine you are reaching down inside your body and pulling out all that dark, ugly stuff—all that shame and self-blame.
4. Now imagine you are throwing all that dark ugliness at the abuser, where it belongs.
5. Open your eyes and make a throwing motion with your arms. Say out loud as you do it, "Take back your shame. It's not mine. It's yours." Do this until you can feel the truth of what you are saying.

In addition to pushing away shame, anger also helps in the separation/individuation process, which we will discuss later in this chapter. Anger separates people. Think about it; when you are angry with someone, you don't usually want to be close to that person. In fact, if you are paying attention to your body messages, you will notice that when you are angry with someone it causes your body to turn away or pull away from that person. You may feel uncomfortable even sitting next to the person or having the person touch you. Anger also helps in the separation process because it empowers us and motivates us to make changes. If you allow yourself to become angry with your parents for their mistreatment of you, it can give you the courage to begin to break some of your unhealthy emotional ties to them.

Getting Past Your Fear of Anger

You may be reluctant to express your righteous anger toward your parents because you are afraid of your anger, the most threatening and frightening of all our emotions. But it is important to realize that your fear of anger has kept you imprisoned in the past, afraid to stand up to those who have hurt you and afraid to go forward. If you can conquer your fear of anger, you can rise above the status of victim to that of survivor. The following suggestions can help:

- Identify any myths you have about anger and your right to express it.

- Identify the beliefs in your family that prevented the expression of anger.

- Whose style of anger have you adopted? How did this person come to be a role model for you? How effective a role model is this person?

Anger itself is not a negative emotion. It is what we do with our anger that determines whether it is negative or positive. If we go about spewing out our anger on innocent people, it becomes negative. If we hold anger in and turn it against ourselves, it also becomes negative. But if we find constructive ways of releasing it and safe places to let out our anger, it becomes a positive force in our lives, creating energy, motivation, assertiveness, empowerment, and creativity.

Anger is energy, a motivating force that can empower you to feel less helpless. By releasing it you will find that you rid yourself of the physical and emotional tension that has sapped your energy—energy that you could otherwise use to motivate yourself to change. Anger can motivate you to set and keep boundaries with your parents today, as well as with other people in your life. The more you express your anger, the less afraid of it you will be. Anger can be your way out—take it.

Exercise: Constructive and Safe Ways to Identify and Express Your Anger

1. Write down all the negative ways the emotional abuse or neglect affected you. This may take some thought and some time. Allow yourself to feel your righteous anger at having to suffer in these ways.

2. Write about any connections you can make between your low self-esteem, your tendency to be self-critical, and your unexpressed anger.

3. Write about any connections you can make between your experiences of depression and your unresolved anger.

4. Write about any connections you can make between your experiences of anxiety and your unresolved anger.

5. Talk about your angry feelings to someone you trust—someone who will just listen and understand without trying to rescue you or talk you out of your anger.

6. Write a letter to the parent or caregiver who abused or neglected you, expressing your hurt and anger. Don't censor yourself; let yourself say all the negative, hateful things that are going through your head. This letter is only meant as a catharsis—do not give it to the person. You can choose to keep the letter, tear it up, or burn it.

7. Role-play your anger. Have an imaginary conversation with the person you are angry with. Tell that person exactly what you feel: don't hold anything back. It may help to look at a picture of the person or to imagine that the person is sitting in a chair across from you. If you are still afraid of this person, imagine he or she is tied up and gagged and cannot hurt you or say anything to you.

8. Find a creative outlet for your anger. For example, paint the rage you feel when you think about the treatment you received; make a clay representation of your abusive or neglectful parent and then destroy it.

9. If you need something more physical, express your anger through dance, scream into a pillow, or scream in the shower (if you can do so without anyone hearing you).

10. Find a physical activity that helps you release your anger energy in a safe way. Good examples are running, playing basketball, or going to a batting cage and hitting some balls. If you tend to suffer from explosive anger, avoid aggressive or competitive sports such as boxing, wrestling, or hockey, as they may actually reinforce aggressive behavior instead of releasing anger. Instead, find physical activities that make you feel calm and relaxed, such as walking, swimming, or running.

Identify and Counter Negative Core Beliefs

If a child is constantly told, "You're no good," he ends up believing it. If he is told he will never amount to anything, he will most likely grow up to prove his parents right. Children who were emotionally abused or deprived almost always internalize the negative parental messages they received. In order to eliminate these negative internal messages we need to identify their presence.

Parents communicate negative messages to their children in various ways. Some are overtly critical of their child or his behavior. Comments such as "You're stupid," "You're a lost cause," and "You're an embarrassment to me" are common examples of messages passed on by emotionally abusive parents.

Other kinds of negative and debilitating beliefs are communicated in less obvious ways. For example, in response to the rejection or abandonment you experienced as a child, you may have come to see yourself as unworthy or flawed. If your parents did not mirror back your value, you find it difficult to see value in yourself.

In my case, my mother passed on to me the negative core belief that I did not deserve good things. Whenever good things happened to me when I was a little girl, my mother would either warn me that something bad was going to happen or she would do something to make me feel bad.

The most powerful experience of this message occurred when I was fifteen and a junior in high school. My first two years in high school hadn't been very good for me. I had transferred from another school district and didn't know many people. Because we were poor and my mother hadn't taught me how to take care of myself, I didn't look as attractive as I could have. But by my junior year I had learned a little from classes in home economics and from watching how the other girls dressed, and I began to dress more appropriately. I had also made some new friends—enough, in fact, that a friend of mine and I were able to create our own lunch table in the cafeteria, a safe harbor in the midst of chaos. I was doing well in school and had gained the respect of some of the more popular kids in my classes. When two seniors asked me to join their YWCA club I was honored. Things were definitely looking up.

On one particular day, I was feeling especially great. My English teacher had complimented me in front of the entire class on a term paper I had written. She said I was a very good writer and that I should seriously consider it as a career. I remember feeling so proud. I respected this teacher very much, and to have her praise me in front of everyone gave me the kind of validation I seldom received in my life. After school that day I was elected president of my YWCA club. Again, this was incredible validation for me.

I sailed all the way home, buoyed up by these validations. I relived the experience of my teacher praising me over and over in my head and felt the warm glow of acceptance and admiration from the club members. It was my mother's day off and so I bounded into the apartment, eager to tell her about both of my successes. I don't remember what she said about them—certainly she did not praise me or tell me anything positive.

I telephoned my best friend and told her what had happened in class and continued to feel good about myself for the rest of the afternoon and into the evening. I don't know how I was acting, but clearly my mother didn't like it. All I do remember is that my mother, who was sitting on the couch drinking beer, said to me, "You really think you're something, don't you?" I stopped short, not knowing what she was talking about. "You really think you're something because your teacher praised you and because you're president of your stupid club. Well, let me tell you something. Let me tell you who you really are," she said in a mocking tone. "You're illegitimate. You were an unwanted child who ruined my life."

I stood there, shocked, not quite comprehending what she was telling me, but feeling wounded by her words. The word *illegitimate* rang in my ears. In those days, the mid-sixties, being an illegitimate child was still very shameful. I remember feeling that I was going to pass out as hurtful emotions passed over me like a dark cloud.

I sank to the couch as my mother proceeded to tell me, for the first time, the truth about my father and my birth. My mother was not married to my father when I was conceived. In fact, she was actually still legally married to another man, even though she had deserted him. She never told my father about me but left town as soon as she discovered she was pregnant. In the moments that followed, my entire concept of who I was changed. I had always felt different and less than others because I had no father, because my mother was so much older than other mothers, and because we were so poor. Now I had another reason to feel inadequate: I was illegitimate. And even though I had always felt unwanted and guilty about my existence, now it was confirmed—I *was* unwanted and I had ruined my mother's life. Needless to say, all the good feelings I'd had about being acknowledged that day absolutely disappeared. Although my mother had not physically slapped me in the face this time, I felt slapped "down to size" nevertheless.

The juxtaposition of the events of this day had a profound effect on me. For many years I could not experience joy or the feeling of success without fearing that something bad was going to happen to me—that I was going to get slapped down to size.

I vividly remember the day when I was finally able to let go of the fear that something bad was going to happen to me every time I felt good. It was about fifteen years ago. I was driving home from work, feeling good about the work I had done that day with clients. I realized that my life was going really well—that for the first time in a long time I wasn't weighted down by some kind of problem. Suddenly I was seized with an overwhelming fear. I just knew that something bad was going to happen to me. But then another feeling slowly began to seep into my consciousness and I heard a voice inside my head say, "No, nothing bad is going to happen. Just because you are happy right now doesn't mean that something bad will follow." I continued my ride home feeling free of the fear that would have normally gripped me, and free to feel the contentment I was experiencing.

That was not the end of the story. For many years I continued to battle with another version of this problem. Instead of consciously fearing that something bad would always follow something good, I had a tendency to do something to hurt myself whenever something wonderful happened to me. For example, several years ago I began rewarding myself with a massage every other week. But after having my body taken care of and feeling so good, I noticed that I would eat too much at night. I often "slapped myself down" in the same way my mother slapped me down on that horrible day.

Negative parental messages like the one I received from my mother cause us to develop certain core beliefs about life and about ourselves, including basic assumptions about our value in the world. Core beliefs about yourself can determine to what degree you perceive yourself as worthy, competent, loved, safe, powerful, and autonomous. The core belief I developed from experiences with my mother was that I didn't deserve good things. After all, echoing my mother's words, "Who did I think I was?" This belief colored my perceptions of myself to such an extreme extent that whenever something good happened to me, I immediately sabotaged it in some way.

Examples of Negative Core Beliefs

Negative beliefs and negative thought patterns can continue to affect your identity and self-concept unless you consciously work on changing them. In chapter 2 I listed the common beliefs created by the seven types of emotionally abusive parents. Following are some other common examples of thought patterns that people who were deprived and/or abused have. The underlying beliefs that support these thoughts patterns are in italics. Make a note of any of the negative beliefs that you relate to.

1. I can never trust that anything good will last. It will either end or go away. *People are not trustworthy and neither is life—both will disappoint you and let you down.*

2. I have no control over my life or what happens to me. I just have to accept whatever happens and try to make the best of it. *What I said or did never stopped my parents (or other caregivers) from abusing me. Nothing I say or do makes a difference, so why bother?*

3. I am helpless to effect changes in my life. *I was a victim in my childhood and will always be a victim.*

4. I am to blame for the pain I feel and for my problems. *If I had not done things to make my parents angry or done things wrong, I wouldn't have been punished.*

5. The only time I feel good about myself is when I am giving to other people or helping other people. *The only value I have is what I can do for others.*

6. I cannot be assertive, because then other people will not like me. *If I speak up about what I need, other people will think I am selfish.*

7. I should never tell anyone when I feel hurt, disappointed, or angry, because I will make the other person feel hurt or angry. *I am responsible for other people's feelings.*

8. I should never talk about what goes on in my family, because I am being disloyal. *Secrets are to be kept and never talked about—even with other family members.*

9. I can't trust my perceptions. *My parents always told me that what I thought or believed was wrong.*

Core beliefs about yourself are the foundation of your self-esteem. To a large degree, they dictate what you can and cannot do—in other words, they form the basis of the rules you live your life by. Generally speaking, *negative* core beliefs dictate what you *can't* do, for example, "I shouldn't even bother to get that job. No one is going to want to hire me because I'm not a good communicator." On the other hand, *posi-*

tive core beliefs encourage you by *affirming* your abilities, as in, "I know I can pass this course. I'm smart and I'm capable of learning even difficult concepts if I put my mind to it."

Negative parental messages also set us up to have unreasonable expectations of ourselves and others. In my case, I desperately wanted the approval of others (especially my mother). I came to believe that if I was exceptionally "good," I would finally get that approval. This led me to have unreasonable expectations of myself in terms of how hard I worked at being a good person and at achieving success.

EXERCISE: YOUR CORE BELIEFS

1. Think about the way your parents treated you as a child. Based on this treatment, what false beliefs and unreasonable expectations of yourself and life do you think you developed? Completing the following sentences will help you see clearer.

   When my father _____ ("ignored me", "criticized me"), it led me to believe that I _____ ("am unimportant," "am incompetent").

2. Continue to complete this sentence until you have no more responses:

   When my father _____, it led me to believe that I _____.

3. Now complete the following sentence. Once again, continue until you have no more responses.

   When my mother _____ ("expected too much of me"), it led me to _____ ("expect too much of myself").

4. Make a list of the beliefs you developed due to your parents' treatment of you when you were growing up, using your answers from the sentence-completion exercise and the preceding examples of negative beliefs.

5. Make a separate list of the unreasonable expectations you have, based on the ways your parents treated you and your early childhood experiences.

Identifying these false beliefs and unreasonable expectations is the first step to exorcising them from your mind. If you are still uncertain as to what your false beliefs and unreasonable expectations are, the assignment at the end of the chapter will help.

It may seem to us that our negative beliefs and unreasonable expectations of ourselves and about life are permanently installed in our brains and that changing our minds about these negative beliefs is near to impossible. But the truth is that it is possible to change even the most negative, unhealthy, and destructive beliefs. In the next two chapters you will be offered more exercises and activities that will help you in this process.

Changing your core beliefs can take a great deal of time and effort, but it is definitely worth it. By doing so you will be able to alter your view of yourself and the world in a significant way. Earlier I wrote about how having emotionally abusive parents is like looking at yourself in a fun-house mirror, causing you to see yourself in a distorted way. Getting rid of negative core beliefs about yourself is like replacing the fun-house mirror with a nondistorting one. Instead of seeing yourself as a tiny monster, you see yourself as normal sized and proportioned.

Psychological Truths of the Week

- Problems with low self-esteem and poor body image are often caused by negative parental messages communicated through emotional abuse, neglect, or smothering.

- The only real alternative to self-judgment is knowing the truth about who you are. If you have a deep belief that you are worthless, you must discover where that belief came from and why you believe it is true.

Mirror Therapy Assignment #5: Your Self-Talk Diary

This week begin to keep a self-talk diary or journal in which you record your self-statements or inner monologue whenever you feel angry, sad, depressed, guilty, and so on. It will no doubt be difficult at first to catch yourself in the act of thinking negative thoughts, because they are often so ingrained. It might help if you try to identify situations in which your self-esteem is particularly low, such as when you feel incompetent, stupid, or especially unattractive. Carrying your self-talk diary around with you will help you record your feelings and self-statements while they are fresh in your mind. Describe the *situation* ("I went to a business mixer and no one approached me to talk"), your *self-statements* ("You're so fat no one wants to talk to you"), and how you are *feeling* because of the situation ("ugly"). Here's what your self-talk diary pages might look like:

Date: September 25

Situation	Self-Statement	Feeling
Boss didn't like my report	"I'm so stupid. I'm always messing up"	Incompetent
Wasn't able to get an erection	"You're not even a man"	Inadequate
Locked keys in car	"What an idiot, you'd forget your head if it wasn't attached to you."	Worthless

6

Emotionally Separating
from Your Parents

When I say "I" I mean a thing absolutely unique,
not to be confused with any other.

—UGO BETTI

There is no ache more Deadly than the striving to be oneself.

—YEVGENIY VINOKUROV

I was supposed to become her, if I had turned out according to
plan. I was trained to repeat her life, daughter becoming wife
becoming mother. I carry her fears and limitations in weights
around my wrists and ankles. My body was molded first by her
own body and then by the words she wrapped around my feelings.

—LOUISE M. WISECHILD, *The Mother I Carry*

ONE OF THE PRIMARY REASONS adults who were neglected or emotionally abused as children continue to buy into their parents' negative
beliefs is that they are still too emotionally tied to their parents and
have not completed the individuation process. Individuation is the act
of becoming a separate person from one's parents and one's family.

Those who have a history of neglect or abuse tend to remain enmeshed with their family of origin out of the desperate desire to get what they did not get when they were children. But the sad truth is that most of us will never get from our parents what we missed out on in childhood. We need to accept that we have to grow up, even if we don't feel emotionally equipped to do so.

You may have worked hard to be different from your parents, and you may have been on your own for quite some time, but this doesn't mean that you have become separate from them emotionally. This takes more than just getting older—it takes emotional maturity and conscious effort on your part.

In healthy families, emotional separation takes place naturally and gradually. It begins during the rapprochement phase referred to earlier (from two to four years of age), when a child first discovers she is a separate self from her parents. During this time it is essential that a child have experiences that validate her ability to be separate without feeling abandoned. Even though a child has a mounting need to find her own place in the world, she still requires physical caretaking from her parents as well as needing to be loved by them.

But sometimes parents and other caretakers have a difficult time allowing both independence and dependence. For example, Marie preferred to play alone and spent a lot of time in her room instead of sitting with the family at night and watching television. This hurt her mother's feelings. Because her mother took it personally and felt rejected by Marie (as is often the case with smothering parents), she distanced herself from her daughter each time she went into her room at night. By doing this, Marie's mother sent her the message that it was not okay for her to have a separate self.

Some parents only feel comfortable when their children are dependent or needy, and they may discourage any signs of independence in them. This is especially true of smothering or emotionally incestuous parents. For example, when a child is beginning to walk or to explore the world, a healthy parent will respond with appropriate support and encouragement, applauding each small success. An insecure or anxious parent, on the other hand, may respond by inhibiting her child's efforts and by ignoring or withdrawing from her child.

Adolescence is another period of accelerated growth and a push for independence. During this typically tumultuous time, most adolescents are extremely rebellious, insisting on doing things their own way and rejecting their parents' suggestions, values, and sometimes, rules. They are inexplicably angry with their parents, blaming them for anything and everything that goes wrong in their lives. This is actually healthy, since anger helps adolescents to separate from their parents and discover their own identities.

Unfortunately, neglected or abused children often do not go through adolescence in a healthy way. They are often too afraid of their parents or too afraid of rejection to rebel against their parents' values. And they are often too caught up in trying to gain their parents' approval and love to work on developing a separate identity from them. Abusive parents often do not want their children to separate, or they lack the skills to help them separate in a healthy way.

How do you go about emotionally separating from your parents and completing the individuation process if you have yet to do so? How do you replace your parents' distorted mirror with a more accurate one? Emotionally separating from them may include any or all of the following: providing yourself with the encouragement and support you did not receive from your parents, expressing the anger you have been afraid to express, acknowledging your unmet needs, and facing the fact that the time for getting those needs met by your parents is over. It also includes grieving for all the pain, rejection, abandonment, and betrayal you experienced at the hands of your parents or other caretakers.

Individuation also involves resolving your relationship with your parents in a conscious way as opposed to constantly reenacting the relationship with others, namely your spouse and children. One of the ways that adults who were abused or neglected as children create a false sense of connection with their parents is by unconsciously repeating their lives. If they do what their parents did, they do not have to feel separate from them. It is as if they are living their parents' lives instead of their own. In this way they never have to become separate people and take responsibility for their own lives.

Enmeshment

Many survivors have a very difficult time acknowledging the abuse or neglect they suffered at the hands of their parents and an especially difficult time becoming angry with them. This is partly because they don't want to have to face the truth and come out of denial, but it is also because they are too enmeshed with their parents. *Enmeshment* is a term used in psychology to describe an unhealthy dependence on another person. In order for some people to admit what was done to them, they need to develop their own identities separate from their parents (or other abusers).

We remain enmeshed with our parents in the following ways:

- By continuing to stay in denial about how they treated us
- By withholding our anger concerning their neglectful or abusive treatment
- By completely taking on their values and beliefs without any analysis or questioning
- By replicating their behavior and becoming just like them
- By trying to be the exact opposite of them
- By working hard to never anger them or otherwise risk their rejection
- By deliberately doing things that will make them angry or create conflict with them
- By not setting healthy limits and boundaries with them

The following information and suggestions will help you counter the ways you have remained enmeshed.

Declare Your Independence

You began to declare your independence when you started to face the truth about your parents and other family members and the negative role their behavior has played in your life. When you began to give voice to this recognition by expressing your righteous anger, the emotional separation process accelerated. Standing up to your parents and saying no to them (perhaps for the first time) are other ways of declaring your independence from your parents and their ways of doing things. This action can be empowering and exhilarating. It allows you to see how different you are from the people you identified with as a child and how different you are from the mirror they projected onto you.

Declaring your independence does not involve denying the emotional impact your parents have had on you, however. By denying your parents' role in shaping your personality you risk denying a part of yourself. It is inevitable that you will take on many of your parents' characteristics. After all, their influence on you, both genetically and environmentally, is the most profound influence you will ever experience. Separation includes acknowledging how you are similar to your parents as well as how you are different from them, for many of the traits that you have inherited from your parents are no doubt very positive.

Some people spend most of their lives trying desperately to become different from one or both of their parents. Ironically, the ones who work hard to become different are actually just as emotionally tied to their parents as the ones who attempt to emulate them. Their focus on being different from their parent can actually prevent them from becoming themselves. By focusing too much energy on being different from your parent, you take away energy from discovering who you really are.

Exercise: The Good and the Bad

1. List all the ways you feel you are similar to your parents.

2. List all the ways you feel you are different from your parents.

3. Write about how these two lists make you feel. Are you disturbed by how many similarities there are? Are you proud of the differences?

Question Your Parents' Values and Beliefs

You do not have to automatically take on your parents' or your family's values and beliefs, especially if they contribute to your neglecting or abusing yourself. In fact, you can be the first one in your family to question values and beliefs that until now have been taken for granted to be true. The following exercise will help you begin:

EXERCISE: YOUR PARENTS' BELIEFS/YOUR BELIEFS

1. Make a list of your parents' beliefs and values that you agree with.
2. Make a list of the beliefs and values you disagree with.
3. Consider which of your parents' beliefs and values are conducive to self-neglect or self-abuse.
4. Which of the values and beliefs from item 3 have you taken on as your own?

Set Healthy Limits and Boundaries

If you have continued to be controlled or manipulated by your parents, or if you have remained too dependent on them, you will need to set boundaries and limits in order to individuate from them. It can be painful to see your parents' pain and disappointment when you begin to tell them no—no, you aren't going to do as they suggest; no, you aren't coming over now; no, you aren't going to become what they wanted you to become. You may be afraid they will say, "In that case, to hell with you" in response to your show of autonomy. Your parents may, in fact, initially become quite angry when you first begin to set limits and boundaries with them. They may even become insulting, bitter, or threatening when you stand up to them and tell them you are going to run your life your way. But do not allow these reactions to throw you off your course.

Complete Your Unfinished Business

Completing your unfinished business with your parents or other abusers can include any or all of the following: expressing and getting past your anger, confronting your abusers, resolving your relationship, and forgiveness.

Getting Past Your Anger

Resentment is the most frequent kind of unfinished business. Although it is natural and normal for you to feel resentment (which translates into *anger*) toward your parents, you will need to get past your anger if you are to emotionally separate from them. When we remain angry with someone, we stay emotionally tied to them in a very negative way. We continue to feel victimized by them, investing a tremendous amount of energy in blaming them. While anger is a natural, healthy emotion when ventilated properly, blame is a wasted and negative experience. The difference between anger and blame is that blaming keeps you caught up in the problem, while releasing your anger constructively allows you to work through the problem.

If you have not successfully worked through your anger toward your abusers, refer back to the exercise given earlier in chapter 5 on constructively identifying and releasing your anger.

Confrontations

Confronting your parents or other abusers has many benefits. It can help you emotionally disconnect from people with whom you continue to have an unhealthy emotional connection and help you resolve or bring closure to the relationships that plague you most (with your parents, siblings, or other abusers).

Confronting the ones who hurt you enables you to take back your power, proving to yourself that you are no longer going to allow anyone to frighten, control, or mistreat you. It provides an opportunity to set the record straight, to communicate what you need from now on. It gives the other person another chance to make amends and to treat you better now.

A confrontation is a way of declaring the truth, of standing up to those who have hurt you and telling them how they hurt you and how you feel about them. It is not an attack and it is not meant to alienate them. It is also not an argument. Its purpose is not to change the other people or to force someone to admit that she was wrong in the way she treated you.

Confronting is different from releasing your anger. Although your confrontation may include expressing your anger along with your other feelings, it is generally important that you have released a great deal of your anger in constructive ways before you confront, because you will be better able to communicate your feelings in a strong, clear, self-assured manner. You will also be less likely to explode or lose control. It is strongly recommended that you write an "anger letter" before you do your confronting. From this letter you can glean the material for your confrontation.

Practice your confrontation by writing it down, speaking into a tape recorder, or just talking out loud. You can practice with a friend or a therapist. Use the following format as a guide. You may then pick and choose which points you wish to include in your actual confrontation.

1. List the neglectful or abusive behaviors this person inflicted upon you.

2. Explain how you felt as a result of these behaviors.

3. List the effects these behaviors had on you, both as a child and as an adult, and how your life has been affected.

4. List everything you wanted from this person at the time.

5. List what you want from the person now.

There are several ways to conduct your confrontation: face-to-face, by telephone, or by letter or e-mail. Face-to-face confrontations are the most advantageous but sometimes not possible due to distance, or because you are not prepared to see someone in person. Choose the method that suits your needs and trust that whichever one you choose will work out.

Before you choose to actually confront someone in person, consider the following:

1. Decide whether you would like to have someone come with you for support. If you are apprehensive about violence or loss of control, you may need to have a third party present—even if it is your own rage or loss of control that you fear.

2. Set some ground rules for the confrontation and determine how you will express these to your parent. Here are some examples: "I want you to hear me out before you respond"; "I don't want you to interrupt me or stop me until I am finished"; "I don't want you to defend, justify, or rationalize—just listen. You'll get your chance to respond later."

3. Even if the person does agree to your ground rules, be prepared for any of the following, both during and after your confrontation:

   Denial: "I don't remember," "That never happened," "You're exaggerating," "You're lying."

   Blame: "You were such a demanding child," "I had to do something to control you," "You wanted it—you came on to me," "Why didn't you tell me?"

   Rationalizations: "I did the best I could," "Things were really tough," "I tried to stop drinking but I couldn't," "I was afraid to leave your father—how were we going to make it?"

   Self-pity: "I have enough problems without this," "You just don't understand how hard it was for me," "I'm too old (or sick) to take this."

   Guilt: "This is what we get after all we did for you?" "Nothing was ever enough for you," "How could you do this to me?

4. Make sure you have supportive people to talk to before and after the confrontation.

5. Be prepared to end the confrontation whenever you feel it is no longer effective, beneficial, or safe—if you feel threatened or fear you are losing control, if your parent is too busy defending himself to really hear you, or if the confrontation has turned into a shouting match.

Don't set yourself up with the false hope that your parent or other family member will suddenly see the error of her ways and apologize profusely. In fact, you can expect her to deny, claim to have forgotten, project the blame back onto you, or get very angry. Give the person time to think about what you have said. Don't assume that just because she didn't apologize on the spot she didn't take what you said seriously and might not apologize in some way later on.

No matter how the confrontation turns out, consider it successful simply because you had the courage to do it. This confrontation symbolizes the beginning to a change in the balance of power in your relationship and is a significant act of individuation on your part.

Resolve Your Relationships with Your Parents and Other Abusers

Unresolved relationships will continue to bother you and negatively affect your life until you get things out in the open, giving room for healing. Resolving a relationship with a parent or other abusers may involve any or all of the following: forgiveness, reconciliation, temporary separation, or "divorce."

Forgiveness

There is no doubt that forgiveness frees us. Forgiveness has the power to heal our bodies, our minds, and our spirits—our very lives. But we need to make sure we aren't forgiving just because we think it is the right thing to do or because we are giving in to pressure from others. And we need to make sure that we are not just using forgiveness as another form of denial.

True forgiveness occurs only when we allow ourselves to face the truth and to feel and release our emotions, including our anger, about what was done to us. It is completely premature to forgive if you haven't even acknowledged that you were harmed. Alice Miller notes that when children are asked to forgive abusive parents without first experiencing their emotions and their personal pain, the forgiveness process becomes another weapon of silencing. The same is true of adults who rush to forgiveness. Many people have been brainwashed into submission by those who insist that they are "less than" if they don't forgive.

Many people think that forgiving someone who hurt them is the same as saying that what happened to them was okay or that it didn't hurt them. But forgiveness doesn't mean that what happened was okay. It simply means that we are no longer willing to allow that experience to adversely affect our lives. Ultimately, forgiveness is something we do for ourselves. The information in chapter 7 will further help you to forgive your parents.

Reconciliation

Even though you may have forgiven your abuser, you may not feel safe to be around him. Many survivors of childhood abuse have stopped seeing their parents or other family members as a way to protect themselves from further abuse. This is especially true for those who confronted their abusers in the past but did not achieve positive results. If your abuser is not open to looking at what he has done to damage you, or continues to abuse you in the same way he did when you were a child, or presents a threat to your children, you may need to continue to separate from him or even divorce him (for more information on this, refer to my book *Divorcing a Parent*).

On the other hand, if your abuser has shown some capacity for understanding your pain and some willingness to take responsibility for his actions—however small that capacity and willingness may seem—there may be hope for the relationship. This is also the case if you have noticed that your abuser has been open to your attempts at setting limits and boundaries.

Before you reconcile, ask yourself the following questions:

1. Am I strong enough to be around this person without losing ground in my recovery?

2. Can I maintain a sense of emotional separation from this person when I am in his presence?

3. Am I strong enough to set appropriate limits and boundaries so that I do not allow myself to be abused again?

4. Am I being pressured into reconciliation (by other family members, by my spouse, by guilt, or by my religious beliefs) before I am actually ready?

5. Is this person ready to reconcile with me? Is she still angry with me for being angry with her, for not having seen her for a while, or for bringing the abuse out in the open? (If so, she may need more time to heal and forgive, no matter how forgiving you might feel.)

If you can't answer yes to questions 1, 2, 3, and 5 and no to question 4, you may need to wait a while before attempting a reconciliation.

Facing the Pain and Confusion of Emotional Separation

Emotional separation often involves emotional pain. It can be painful to face the truth about your parents, to question their beliefs and the lessons they taught you, to stand up to them, or to disagree with them today. Separation brings losses, and even though they are necessary losses, they are still painful. You may have to give up the false hope that your parents will one day be the kind you have longed for and deserve. This loss can be especially painful.

Emotional separation can also create internal conflict. You may realize that taking care of yourself and being true to yourself will necessitate going against your parents' wishes and beliefs. This may cause you to feel you are being disloyal to them. You may vacillate between conflicting emotions such as wanting to recapture a real or imagined sense of family closeness and a desire for revenge or compensation from your parents. At one moment you may feel like you want nothing to do with your parents or other abusive family members and at another moment you may worry that you might be disowned. It is especially challenging to distinguish between the negative internalized messages of your parents and the healthy messages of your true voice.

Emotional separation involves the ability to hold the tension of two opposites. Although it is important to face the truth about your parents' mistreatment of you and to allow yourself to be angry with them, it is also important to realize that your parents were themselves mistreated. It is important to understand that you didn't deserve the way you were mistreated and neither did your parents deserve the way they were mistreated. Although your parents were not responsible for what happened to them as children, they *are* responsible for what they did to you.

You will find that you will continue to grieve over the losses of your childhood throughout the separation process and that it will be a significant part of your healing. Your parents no doubt experienced losses in their childhoods but were not able to grieve over them. This contributed to their repeating what was done to them. By facing your grief, you reduce your own need to abuse others.

While emotional separation often takes time and the support of others, such as supportive friends, family members, therapists, or self-help groups, people who have been able to complete these steps report feeling as though they have finally taken the reins in their lives.

Psychological Truths of the Week

Those who have a history of abuse or neglect tend to remain enmeshed with their parents out of a desperate desire to get what they did not get when they were children.

MIRROR THERAPY ASSIGNMENT #6

1. Review this chapter and write down which aspect of emotionally separating from your parents you are currently working on (declaring your independence, questioning your parents' values and beliefs, setting healthy limits and boundaries, completing your unfinished business, or resolving your relationship with your parents or other abusers).

2. Note how long you have been working on this phase, what tools you've used, and what you feel you still need to do in order to complete this step.

3. Write about which step you have the most anxiety or fear about, or which step seems to be the most difficult for you.

7

Quieting and Countering
Your Inner Critic

It's hard to fight an enemy who has outposts in your head.

—SALLY KEMPTON

Let me listen to me and not to them.

—GERTRUDE STEIN

PEOPLE WHO WERE EMOTIONALLY ABUSED or neglected in childhood tend to have much in common, including a tendency to continually evaluate themselves, judge themselves harshly, and set unreasonable expectations and standards for themselves. Unfortunately, even though these tendencies may be a direct result of how your parents treated you, they don't go away just because you have successfully separated from your parents. These tendencies can hang on, a regretful legacy of the childhood abuse or neglect you experienced.

My client Connie describes herself this way: "I'm an educated woman but I feel so incompetent and stupid most of the time. I constantly compare myself with other people and always end up feeling inferior in some way. I'm constantly amazed how other people seem to be able to speak up and not worry about whether what they say is going to be negatively judged by others, because I'm always afraid I'll say something that will let other people know just how incompetent I really am. Other people tell me that they are impressed with how much I know and what a good job I do, but I don't trust others' assessment of me. I always think they just feel sorry for me and are trying to build me up. I can't take in their compliments—even those from close friends. No matter what other people tell me, based on my own criteria, I'm just not good enough." Connie can't relax and enjoy her life, because she has a powerful inner critic who dominates her every action.

If you identified with some or all of Connie's feelings, you also have a powerful inner critic. The following questionnaire will help you determine just how powerful your inner critic is.

QUESTIONNAIRE: DETERMINING THE STRENGTH OF YOUR INNER CRITIC

1. Do you spend a great deal of time evaluating your performance, your appearance, your abilities, or your past history?

2. Do you set very high standards for yourself?

3. Is it difficult to live up to the standards you use to judge yourself?

4. Do you give yourself little breathing room to make mistakes?

5. Is your underlying sense of self often determined by your beliefs regarding what is right and wrong?

6. Is your sense of self often determined by whether you have met your own or others' standards?

7. Do you spend a great deal of time worrying that you have done something wrong?

8. Are you continually plagued by critical messages inside your head that you are unable to quiet?

9. Do you constantly compare yourself to others or to the success of others?

10. Are you often envious of others' successes or achievements?

If you answered yes to many of these questions, your life and your experience of life are being dominated by your inner critic.

Your Inner Critic

A person raised by nurturing, supportive parents normally develops an inner critic who represents internalized rules and consequences. This inner critic causes him to feel "signal anxiety" when contemplating an action that goes against his value system, as well as guilt and sometimes depression if he actually transgresses. In this way a healthy inner critic provides self-imposed punishment that keeps a person's behavior under the control of his or her system of morality. But anxiety, guilt, and depression are kept within reasonable bounds, because his conscience is modeled on his parents' reasonable attitudes. We internalize the inner critic and its standards to keep our parents with us and to give ourselves a sense of protection, safety, and imagined power over ourselves and reality.

People who have been neglected or abused do not have a reasonable inner critic (also known as the superego or the judge). Everyone has a critical inner voice, but people who were emotionally abused or neglected tend to have a more vicious and vocal inner critic. Theirs is a pervasive yet often invisible presence in their lives.

The *pathological critic* is a term coined by the psychologist Eugene Sagan to describe the negative inner voice that attacks and judges us. A loud, verbose inner critic is enormously poisonous to your psychological health—more so, in fact, than any trauma or deprivation you have experienced. We can often heal our wounds and recover from our losses, but the critic is always with us, judging us, blaming us, finding fault in us.

Your inner critic likely treats you with the same lack of understanding and acceptance that your parents did when you were growing up. One of its major jobs is to motivate you toward unreachable ideals. It keeps egging you on to reach that perfect image, never letting you rest or feel satisfied.

Our inner critic's function is to maintain the status quo in two ways: It keeps us away from what it considers to be dangerous or unmanageable parts of ourselves. And it directs us toward whatever ideals it feels will make us an acceptable, successful person. It constantly admonishes us with comments like "Don't do that." Its demands are never-ending and the actual feeling we are left with is "I am not good enough and I never will be."

Your inner critic or judge not only evaluates you according to its own standards, it also constantly compares you with other people. Comparison is closely related to self-judgment—so much so that if you are comparing yourself to someone else, you are also judging yourself. For example, when you are doing well according to one standard, there is always someone who is doing better with whom you can compare yourself. When the inner critic is in control, comparison is always oriented toward determining worth or value—that is, who is "better." If you are different from someone in some way, this means that one of you must be better than the other.

Celia causes herself a great deal of pain by constantly comparing herself to others. For example, when she goes out with her girlfriends, she tends to stay quiet and listen to their stories. As they talk about their children or their latest accomplishments, she feels like such a failure by comparison. Her friends' children seem to be so well adjusted compared to hers, and her friends all seem to be moving up in their careers, while she feels stuck doing the same old job. On the way home, her inner critic reprimands her for being such a bad mother, for not staying in school long enough to get a degree, and for a multitude of other things. By the time she reaches home, she is deep in a depression.

How to Identify Your Inner Critic

The sad truth is that it doesn't matter what you have accomplished in life, how much success you experience, how beautiful or handsome you are, or what efforts you make to raise your self-esteem. If you have a powerful inner critic who chastises you constantly or who discounts your achievements at every turn, your self-esteem will always be low.

The first step to quieting your inner critic is to identify it inside yourself. Your inner critic has many roles. It is that part of you who:

- Creates rules describing how you ought to behave and then screams at you that you are wrong or bad if your needs drive you to violate its rules.
- Blames you for things that go wrong.

- Calls you names such as "stupid," "ugly," and "weak," and makes you believe that the names are true.
- Compares you to others—especially to their achievements and abilities—and finds you wanting.
- Sets impossible standards of perfection.
- Tells you to be the best and that if you are not the best, you are nothing.
- Beats you up for the smallest mistake.
- Keeps track of your failures or shortcomings but doesn't remind you of your accomplishments or strengths.
- Exaggerates your weaknesses by telling you that you *"always* screw up a relationship," *"never* finish what you started," or *"always* say stupid things."

If you were emotionally abused as a child, the chances are high that your inner critic is undermining your self-worth every day of your life. Its voice is so insidious, so woven into the fabric of your very being, that you seldom if ever notice its devastating effects. Your inner critic may be experienced consciously as a thought or a "voice," but most of us are unaware of its habitual activity. Usually we only become aware of it during stressful situations when our shame is activated. For example, when we make a mistake we might hear an inner voice that says something like "What an idiot!" or "There you go again, can't you get anything right?" Before giving an important presentation at work or a speech in front of a class or group, you might hear "You should have prepared more; you're going to make a fool of yourself," or, "Everyone is going to see how nervous you are." Marianne, the woman you met earlier who could not look in the mirror and who suffered from severe depression, described her inner critic like this: "I have a voice inside my head that is relentless. All I hear is, 'You messed up, you didn't do it good enough, you are a failure.'"

Even when you do become aware of the attacks, they can seem reasonable and justified. The judging, critical inner voice seems natural, a familiar part of you. But with every negative judgment, every attack, your inner critic weakens you and tears down any good feelings you have about yourself.

Your inner critic often appears as your own voice, making it seem as if you are the one who has these notions about what is right, what is necessary, or what things mean. But make no mistake about it: the voice you hear is not yours; it belongs to someone who lives inside you, someone you've brought along with you on your life's journey.

By paying attention to your self-judgments, you will begin to realize that they were learned from others. These standards can actually run counter to what you yourself want, feel, or know to be true. Unfortunately, even when you realize the voice is not yours, you cannot separate from it. Hard as you may try not to, you continue to watch yourself, keeping track of your pluses and minuses. You continue to feel watched by those around you and to fear their disapproval, indifference, or rejection. You see your own judge in others as well as hearing it inside yourself. You begin to realize just how little control you have over this judgment process. You are at the mercy of a critical, punitive attitude—a manifestation of your self-distrust and self-hatred.

EXERCISE: YOUR INNER CRITIC/YOUR PARENTS

1. Take some time to write about what your parents wanted for you and from you. Who did they want you to be and why? How did they communicate this, and how did it affect you?

2. Explore the ways in which your inner critic or judge acts like your mother or father. How does the way you relate to yourself reflect how they related to you?

How to Disengage from the Inner Critic

The second step in learning how to disengage from your inner critic or judge is to observe yourself closely while you are experiencing an attack. This will not be an easy task. It will require you to stay present, paying particular attention to your body and your emotional reactions.

1. Pick a self-attack you have recently noticed or one that is very familiar to you (for example, telling yourself you are stupid when you make a mistake or judging yourself harshly in comparison to someone else).

2. If at all possible, find a time and place to be quiet so you can stay with your inner process.

3. Focus your attention away from the outside to the inside— from the judge and its messages to your inner self and how the messages are affecting you. Observing your experience in this way will help you to expose more of the emotional layer of that experience.

4. Once you have become aware of the feelings that are triggered by the attack, either write them down or speak them out loud.

5. By staying with your feelings you may sense that feeling this way is a familiar experience; in fact, it probably has happened many times before. Staying with the feelings that come up will also tend to open you to associated feelings and beliefs about the situation. You may discover a different or deeper understanding of the current attack as you recall earlier experiences. You may notice that you are remembering not only an incident but also an entire cluster of beliefs, body sensations, and other senses such as smell, sound, or visual images. These may all fit together to create a complete experience.

Externalizing Your Inner Dialogue

The critical voice can be activated in any situation in which you find yourself feeling vulnerable or exposed. Once activated, a shaming spiral is set in motion that has a power of its own. Therefore, it is imperative that you externalize this internal dialogue, because it is one of the major ways you keep yourself feeling bad about yourself. It will help you to make the internal dialogue conscious as well as take away some of its power over you.

EXERCISE: EXPOSING YOUR INNER CRITIC

The following is an adaptation of a Gestalt Therapy exercise. It was developed to expose the inner self-critical dialogue that many of us have going on in our heads without realizing it.

1. Sit comfortably with your eyes closed. Imagine that you are facing a mirror and are able to look at yourself as you sit in the chair. Notice how this image—this person who is facing you—is sitting. What are you wearing? What kind of facial expression do you see?

2. Now criticize this image of yourself as if you were talking to another person. It works best if you talk out loud. Tell yourself what you should and shouldn't do. It will help if you begin each sentence with, "You should _____ " or "You shouldn't _____ ." Criticize yourself for several minutes, allowing everything you can think of to come out. Pay close attention to your voice as you criticize yourself.

3. Imagine that you change places with the person facing you—the image of yourself in the mirror. Become the person who was criticized and answer the charges. What do you say in response to these critical comments? What does the tone of your voice express? How do you feel as you respond to these criticisms?

4. Switch roles and become the critic again. As you continue this dialogue, be aware of what you say, how you say it, the tone of your voice, and how you feel. Pause occasionally to listen to your words and to let yourself experience them.

5. Continue to switch roles whenever you feel like it, but continue this dialogue. Notice what is going on inside you as you do this. Notice how you feel both physically and emotionally in each role. Does the voice that is doing the criticism sound like anyone you know? What else are you aware of in this interaction? Continue this dialogue for a few minutes longer and notice any changes as you continue.

6. Sit quietly and review all that transpired during this dialogue. You may wish to write down your feelings and insights. For example, you probably experienced some kind of split or conflict between a powerful, critical, authoritative part of you that demands that you change, and another less powerful part of you that makes excuses, apologizes, or

evades the issue. It may seem that you are divided into a parent and a child. The parent (or, in Gestalt lingo, the "topdog") is always trying to get control to change you into something "better," and the child (or "underdog") is continually evading these attempts to change. You may have noticed that the demanding, critical voice sounded like one of your parents or perhaps someone else in your life who makes demands on you, or another authority figure who controls you.

Talking Back to Your Inner Critic

Your self-esteem has no chance of improving as long as you are constantly being bombarded by the negative messages from your inner critic. One of the most powerful ways of quieting and countering your inner critic is to talk back to him or her. Literally. Just as you would not allow a bully or tyrant to relentlessly criticize you or put you down, you cannot allow your inner critic to continue to wear away at your self-esteem.

Most people are very uncomfortable with the idea of talking back to their inner critic. Because the inner critic is usually created by their parents' messages and may actually take on the form of one of their voices, it may feel as if they are talking back to their parents. If you are still intimidated by your parents, this can be a frightening prospect indeed. If the idea of talking back to your critic scares you, start off slowly, doing it only when you feel particularly brave or strong.

The following phrases have proven to be particularly powerful in silencing an inner critic. Choose the ones that feel good to you, that empower you, that make you feel angry.

- Shut up!
- Stop it!
- This is poison. Stop it!
- Get off my back!
- This is garbage!
- These are lies.

- These are the same lies my mother told me.
- I don't believe you.
- No more put-downs.
- Go to hell!

Catch the critic just as he starts—before he is allowed to weaken you or do much damage. Internally scream at the critic so you can drown him out with your anger. If your inner critic screams back, yell even louder. You may even need to yell out loud. Profanity is perfectly healthy and may empower you further. If you do this whenever you hear your critic's voice, you will find that his attacks will diminish in frequency.

When Your Inner Critic
Becomes a Saboteur

Sometimes it almost seems as if there is a part of us that is bent on sabotaging anything good that comes our way. It especially rears its ugly head when we are trying to make changes to our lives or to break old, negative patterns. I have struggled with a powerful inner saboteur all my adult life. Most recently, it appeared as I began to work on changing the resistance to physical exercise I've had most of my life. After I joined a health club and began swimming regularly and taking aqua aerobics classes, I found that I loved exercising in the water, that in fact it touched something deep in my soul. This encouraged me to step up other types of exercising, and I began to feel better and better about myself. But my inner saboteur wasn't so happy with this turn of events. The following dream shows how it is at work on me, even in my sleep.

In my dream I was with a supportive group of people having fun. I decided to take a shower, which was in the same room. I took off my clothes and got into a glass-enclosed shower. The people around me weren't looking at me and I felt safe in their presence. I was loving the feeling of the water on my naked body, the sensuality of the feel of my skin. I felt very young and very innocent. Suddenly, a preacher came into the shower and started grabbing at my breasts. (I was clearly an adult in the dream, although a younger version of myself.) I was appalled and recoiled away from him. He continued to try to grab me, and I yelled at him to stop. He had a wicked smirk on his face and seemed to be taking pleasure in upsetting me. I continued to back away to get as far away from him as I could, but he kept grabbing at me. The others called to him to stop, but this did no good.

My dream was a clear depiction of my current struggle. The people in the dream represented the support I was receiving from the people at the health club and my personal coach. The shower represented the swimming pool and jacuzzi at my club. And the preacher was clearly my inner saboteur.

Because I was a child of a narcissist who emotionally battered me with criticism and rejection from an early age, I developed what is commonly called a powerful negative *introject,* or *inner saboteur.* Normal parents tend to accept their child even when she does wrong—they condemn her bad behavior without rejecting her. But children of a narcissistic parent (and often those who were highly criticized, manipulated, or rejected) develop a more negative inner critic or negative introject, which is actually an inner representation of the rejecting parent. The negative inner parent or introject lives on in the mind of the adult who was emotionally abused as a child, even when the real parent is absent. The introject embodies the demands the child is supposed to meet in order to gain parental approval, and it reinforces childhood roles and behaviors that were acquired for survival. The introject still threatens to withhold love if the child does not do as he or she wishes. It also embodies the parental rage toward his or her child for failing to meet his standards.

Instead of acting as a healthy monitor, as in the case of a healthy inner critic, the negative introject acts from within as a punishing enemy. It creates such severe anxiety that it paralyzes, producing such powerful guilt that the person feels totally worthless (shamed). Depression, guilt, shame, and inner conflict tear the person apart. It may cause a person to actually victimize himself in much the same way that his parent victimized him—attacking his weaknesses with the same hateful anger and disdain.

There is nowhere to run, no hiding place to get away from this harsh inner voice. But there is a way to quiet this voice. With careful examination, it is possible to root out the influence of the inner saboteur and talk back to it.

As Elan Golumb stated in her book *Trapped in the Mirror*, the negative introject first enters our reality when we are children who desperately need our parents' love. If they are critical or unloving, their disapproving eyes and angry mouths start hurting us from within. As we continue to grow, the negative introject imposes limitations on us. Our true selves may attempt to disagree, but they are inevitably trounced upon by the negative introject. Remember, the negative introject wants to be topdog and, unlike a conscience that leads to comfort through security and limits, it removes security from the self. Despite its negative effect, we believe that by listening to the negative introject we will be able to gain our parents' love.

How to Identify a Negative Introject (Also Called Your Inner Saboteur)

A negative introject or inner saboteur feels like a foreign, attacking entity, because it is partly the voice of your attacking and restrictive (narcissistic) parent whose thinking took up residence in your mind. Little escapes its quest for control. It criticizes you with such comments as "You're a failure" and "Why try?"

Sometimes the saboteur takes the form of a cruel voice inside your head, but usually the cruelty is more silent—and deadly. It is a cruelty that echoes the out-and-out hostility of a narcissistic parent as well as the anger your inner child feels when she is frustrated. This cruelty can cause depression. It can make you discount compliments and distrust affection. Its punitive demands and paralyzing arguments can stop you from trying to change and can cause you to fail at whatever you try to achieve.

The child inside still clings to the hope, however futile, that she will someday be able to gain her parents' love. Because of this, our inner child clings to childish ways and, in many ways, takes over. It can cause us to be addicted to sugar, to procrastinate, to be continually late, to indulge in childhood needs and pleasures while our adult lives fall apart. This is what began happening to me. The more I exercised, the more I began to crave carbohydrates. I had been on a low-carbohydrate diet and had lost quite a lot of weight. I also felt better when I restricted my intake of carbs. But suddenly I was craving them again and not having the willpower to say no.

The normal experience of having an inner critic is that its negative messages can cause us to modify our behavior, but the negative introject or saboteur is indifferent. It doesn't necessarily come in the form of negative messages that can be heard and identified. If you have a saboteur, you may only be able to recognize its influence by carefully noticing what happens whenever you experience pleasure, love, recognition, or success. That's when the saboteur is likely to rear its ugly head, because it feels threatened whenever you experience these things. Your inner saboteur wants to cripple you, keep you from happiness, or even destroy you. It cannot tolerate your feeling or experiencing anything good. What happens when you do experience the good feelings of acceptance, the joy of spontaneity and pleasure, or the pride of accomplishment? Your inner saboteur will find a way to destroy the moment. In my case it was causing me to stuff myself with carbohydrates after experiencing the sensuality of the water while I swam, the connection with my body after I exercised, and the pride in accomplishment when I continually increased my endurance as I learned to swim. It insidiously attacked me by causing me to crave carbohydrates and by quieting my more positive inner critic, who might have reasoned with me to limit my intake, and the healthier part of me, who would signal to me that I was sabotaging the benefits I had gotten by exercising.

The way your saboteur manifests itself is usually related in some way to the type of happiness you are experiencing. For example, it was not a coincidence that my saboteur caused me to overeat whenever I connected to my body in a positive way. If your positive experience is feeling loved or accepted, your saboteur is likely to cause you to behave in a manner that will elicit anger or disapproval from the ones you are close to. For instance, let's say that you are feeling loved by your new boyfriend. Your saboteur doesn't want you to feel loved, so it might cause you to start an argument with your boyfriend, or to flirt with another guy and make your boyfriend angry. Someone who is finally feeling accepted by a group of people might find herself suddenly behaving in a way that causes the group to disapprove of her or turn on her.

Here are some suggestions to help you recognize your inner saboteur:

1. Notice what happens when you experience joy, pleasure, love, recognition, or success.

2. Particularly notice whether you tend to overeat, drink too much, or otherwise indulge whenever you experience any of these positive things—especially when your positive feelings are related to connecting with your body, your sensuality or sexuality, or your emotions.

3. Notice whether you start an argument or push others away whenever you are feeling loved or accepted.

My client Cheryl had a narcissistic mother who never really loved her. Her mother did not want a baby at the time, particularly since she was planning on leaving Cheryl's father. When Cheryl was born, her mother hated the way she looked. She made fun of her to others. By the time Cheryl was two years old, her mother finally decided to leave her father. She left Cheryl with a neighbor couple "just until I get on my feet." That took five years, during which time neither parent came to visit her. When Cheryl was seven years old, her mother arrived at the door one day and announced that she wanted her daughter back. Cheryl was heartbroken about leaving the only mother and father she remembered having. It turned out that the reason her mother suddenly wanted her was that she had remarried and had two small boys, and she needed a babysitter so she could go back to work.

Today, whenever Cheryl feels close to anyone, even for a short time, she immediately pushes the person away by criticizing him or her or by saying something hurtful or insulting. This is her inner saboteur at work.

Doing Battle with Your Inner Saboteur

As Elan Golumb said, "We want to please this uninvited judge that sounds so much like our narcissistic parents. We succumb to its messages, the thoughts that we hate and almost believe. We want to reject such miserable input but lack the foggiest notion of how to do so."

When we fight with our negative introject, we often end up feeling stomped on and exhausted by our efforts. It feels as if we will never win. We take one step forward and then don't just take two steps back but a dozen. We try to ignore the incessant criticism but finally succumb, feeling all the more hopeless in the process.

The power we give to our introject makes it difficult to eradicate, but with deliberate thought and effort, we can put a gag over his mouth:

1. The first step is to identify the introject as something that is foreign to your self. As long as you think of it as something that is a part of you, you are at a disadvantage. If you see it as a non-self, an identification that drives you to unacceptable feelings, behaviors, and roles, you can begin to get the upper hand.

2. Labeling the inner saboteur as a nonself is difficult, because we unconsciously see the introject as an aspect of our narcissistic or overly controlling parent. Loyalty to our parent can undermine our efforts. This is especially true for people who were raised never to put themselves first. In order to rid ourselves of the negative introject and reach our true potential, we must stand alone and face the fact that our parent (particularly a narcissistic parent) cannot now adequately meet our childhood needs any more than he or she could when we were growing up. We must let go of our childish behaviors, fantasies, illusions, and addiction to our unrealizable desire of getting our parents to meet our needs.

3. We need to recognize that our introject uses our parents' values, and if our parents are narcissistic or otherwise emotionally abusive, most of these values cannot lead us to happiness.

4. Because the introject is so harsh, it can never be fully integrated into the personality in the form of a normal conscience, as you would do with an inner critic. This internalized anger with its harsh inner rules needs to be softened and balanced by the experience of parental love in order to develop into a reasonable conscience. Because love is in short supply for

children of narcissists, the negative introject remains destructive. In fact, it takes up the parent's cause from inside the child (and eventually the adult), hating her and telling her not to do and not to be.

I had always felt that my negative introject was a foreigner in my body. In fact, a couple of times in my life I actually heard my negative introject speak to me in a harsh, deep, masculine voice. This made it very clear to me that this voice was not my own. I'll never forget the first time I heard it. I was walking down the street, thinking about how I felt ready to lose weight (I battled with my weight since I was nine years old). As I was silently saying to myself, "I'm really ready, I'm going to do it," I reached the curb. As I stepped off the curb into the street, I heard a voice inside my head say, "F——K you! I'm not going to let you lose weight." This was a powerfully disturbing experience. It felt as if I was possessed. It took many years for me to discover that this voice actually represented my narcissistic mother's voice.

As I mentioned earlier, recently, my inner saboteur returned to try to sabotage my success in getting fit. My dream about the preacher grabbing at me in the shower was a good example. I decided to use this dream and the image of the man grabbing at me to help me fight the negative introject's power. In order to do this, I drew a picture of the preacher and kept the picture with me as a reminder of how present it was in my life.

It was immensely valuable for me to periodically remind myself that my inner saboteur was not me but a foreign entity who had taken up residence inside me. By thinking of it this way, I was able to confront this entity without feeling as if I was attacking a part of myself.

I began by declaring out loud to my saboteur that I was no longer going to allow him to control me. My dialogue went like this: "I want you to know that I'm going to win this battle. I'm no longer going to allow you to control me or sabotage my happiness." I felt incredibly powerful as I spoke these words.

If you choose to engage your saboteur in this manner, be prepared for the consequences. The week following my declaration, my saboteur went into full gear. I became very irritated with a client who arrived late after changing her appointment. Then I noticed that all week I had been driving badly. I'd find myself beginning to swerve off the road for no apparent reason, and once I almost hit the car in front of me because I wasn't paying enough attention. Then I realized that I was banging myself on things. I whacked my head after bending down to get something off the floor, I ran into a table with my hip, and I stubbed my toe. It didn't dawn on me until the end of the week that all these actions were the work of my saboteur. Because my resolve was so great, the realization that it was my inner saboteur at work made me feel all the more determined to win my battle. I continued to talk out loud to him and I continued to swim. Ever so slowly, I noticed that he had begun to weaken. He still rears his ugly head from time to time, but now I am ready. I know what to do.

A word of warning: If you choose to do battle with your inner saboteur, be sure you have plenty of support—either a therapist, a support group, or a 12-step group. If you find yourself feeling overwhelmed or frightened, stop immediately and seek outside help.

Replacing Your Critical Voice with a More Positive, Nurturing Voice

Unfortunately, you cannot permanently quiet your inner critic's or saboteur's voice by challenging him or telling him to shut up. This helps at the time, but eventually his voice will return. What you need to do is replace his voice with another voice—a nurturing inner voice that will substitute the critic's negative messages with positive ones. I will go into detail about how to begin creating this nurturing inner voice in chapter 9.

For now, focus on trying to replace your critic's voice with a positive awareness of your essential worth. This will not be an easy task, since you probably believe that your worth depends on your behavior. Instead of seeing yourself as an empty vessel who is filled up, drop by drop, with your achievements, you need to begin to recognize your intrinsic worth as a human being. This means that you begin to entertain the idea that you are already enough just the way you are. You do not need to achieve anything in order to be of value. Your inner critic would have you believe that you have no intrinsic value, that we are born empty with only the potential for becoming someone worthwhile. But you were born with a tremendous amount of good-ness, wisdom, and strength.

In order to affirm your sense of worth, you need to reconnect with this essential goodness, wisdom, and strength, as we will discuss fur-ther in chapter 8.

Compassion and Self-Acceptance

As Byron Brown, the author of *Soul without Shame*, so eloquently stated, "Compassion is the greatest antidote to the poison of your pathological inner critic." When you are being compassionate toward yourself, you essentially gag your pathological inner critic, who cannot tolerate compassion because it renders him powerless.

Compassion is the essence of self-esteem. When you have com-passion for yourself, you understand and accept yourself the way you are. You tend to see yourself as basically good. If you make a mistake, you forgive yourself. You have reasonable expectations of yourself. You set attainable goals.

Compassion is a skill. That means you can improve it if you already have it, or you can acquire it if you don't. The next time you hear your inner critic chastising you about something you did or did not do, counter this negativity by telling yourself something like "I'm doing the best I can," or "Given my circumstances, this is all I am capable of at this time." Learning to be compassionate toward yourself will also help you make contact with your sense of self-worth.

Unfortunately, to some extent people with a strong inner critic will always be shackled to a negative inner voice. Your job is to diminish the intensity of self-attacks while practicing ways of healthy self-talk. Although you may never be entirely free of an inner voice that says, "What's wrong with you?" or "You're an idiot" whenever you make a mistake, you can create and reinforce the growth of a parallel and even stronger voice that says, "I did the best I could," or "I'm just fine the way I am." You will discover that as your healthy inner voice grows stronger, it will respond more quickly, more forcefully, and more believably to the attacks of your critic. In part three of this book, you will learn more ways to strengthen this healthy inner voice.

Psychological Truths of the Week

- Parental emotional abuse creates a negative inner judge or pathological critic.
- Our inner critic is a mirror that reflects back to us who we think we are. It overrides our inherent intelligence and our direct response to life by superimposing its beliefs about what is real. It is a warped lens that distorts reality. Because of this distorted perception, we come to distrust our intuitive contact with life. Though our inner critic acts as if it were helping us get what we want in life, it actually resists our movement toward growth and development.

MIRROR THERAPY ASSIGNMENT #7: CREATING A NURTURING VOICE

This exercise is an adaptation of an "Imagine" from the Solutions Program (see the appendix at the back of this book for more information).

1. Take a deep breath and begin to go inside.
2. You may become aware of a wall of anger, sadness, fear, or guilt, or you may feel a void inside. Tell yourself that whatever you find inside, it is okay. Continue to focus inside anyway.
3. If you notice a wall of thoughts, step over the wall and begin to sink into yourself more deeply.
4. Focus inside and see if you can find even a fledgling sense of connection with yourself.
5. Bring up a nurturing inner voice. This is not a harsh, critical, or depriving voice, and it is not an overly sweet, indulging voice. It is a warm, kind voice that cherishes you and accepts you for who you are. In time, this voice will become your own, but for now it can be any voice that meets your needs.

PART THREE

Creating a New Mirror

8

Looking Deeper into the Mirror

Discovering the Real You

*What lies behind us and what lies before us are tiny matters
compared to what lies within us.*

—RALPH WALDO EMERSON

*When the mind soars in pursuit of the things conceived in space, it
pursues emptiness. But when the man dives deep within himself, he
experiences the fullness of existence.*

—MEHER BABA

IN ORDER TO CONTINUE to raise your self-esteem and feel better about
yourself you need to find out who you are—not who you were told you
are, not the persona you took on in order to please your parents, but
the real you. Many survivors of emotional abuse and neglect in childhood do not know themselves. They know who their parents have said
they are and they know who they pretend to be, but they don't know
their true selves.

No one can tell you who you are. You are the only one who is capable of determining who your true self is. Your parents' misplaced
labels, distorted perceptions, and negative projections have created a

false image—an image you now need to discard. In its place you will need to discover and create your true self. I say discover, because many of you do not know who you are aside from your parents' mirror. Once this mirror has been smashed, you find that another image does not readily emerge. This means you will need to look deeper inside to begin to find your true reflection.

People who were neglected or abandoned tend to have a fleeting sense of their own identities. It is as if they walk by a mirror and see a reflection of themselves that disappears immediately. Many are in a constant search for clues about who they are, and they often struggle with such a sense of insubstantiality that they feel at times they could actually vanish.

But no matter how fleeting the image or how insubstantial you feel you are, there *is* someone there. You may have to continue to dig to find it under the rubble of your parents' judgments and expectations, or you may have to look deeper into the mirror to find yourself, but sooner or later, with enough focus and patience, you will find the real you. In this chapter we will concentrate on helping you to create a detailed self-portrait. We will start by having you observe your behavior and list your personality traits. I will encourage you to pay attention to your emotions—in particular, what makes you angry, afraid, embarrassed, and sad. Finally, we will focus on helping you discover your *essence* or *true self*—something that is separate from your physical and even your emotional being.

Self discovery requires self-awareness—or an ongoing attention to one's self. In order to truly pay attention to oneself for the purposes of self-discovery, it is important to take on a neutral stance. When you observe yourself in this way, you take in whatever you notice about yourself with impartiality, interest, and curiosity, but you do not *judge* what you observe.

Some do not know their true selves because they are full of conflicts, as was my client Stephanie: "I can't tell who I really am. It keeps changing. One time I think I'm one way only to discover I act in an entirely different way another time." Although all of us change somewhat depending on who we are with and the circumstances we are in, there needs to be an element of consistency and congruence with who we are at any given time. But for people like Stephanie, who tried so hard to be good that she morphed into a different version of herself with each person she was around, finding that core of consistency may be difficult to do. The following suggestions will help you take a close look at yourself and begin to identify who you really are.

EXERCISE: WHO ARE YOU?

1. Closely observe yourself for at least a week. (Notice your behavior, your feelings, and the thoughts that run through your head.) Make notes about what you notice or any insights you may have about yourself. You may also want to use the following questions as a starting-off point:

   • Are you uncomfortable being alone, or are you aware that you need time alone? What do you enjoy doing when you are alone?

   • When do you feel most secure? When do you feel least secure?

   • When do you feel most competent? When do you feel least competent?

   • How do you get your needs met (for example, security, attention, or affection)?

   • Do you do best in a structured environment or with lots of freedom?

2. Start a list of your personality traits. Here's the list of one of my client's: honest, sometimes to a fault ("tell it like it is"), loyal, distrusting, a tendency to worry, overly concerned about what others think of me, a perfectionist, sensitive— get my feelings hurt easily, a tendency to be self-absorbed, sincere, impulsive, obsessive, respectful of others' needs, talented, competent, intelligent, caring. As you continue to observe yourself, you can add to your list.

3. Notice any tendencies you may have to hide your true self from others or yourself, any tendency to pretend you are feeling one thing when you are really feeling another. Also notice such things as how you act with others versus how you are when you are alone.

4. Write a description of yourself based on your observations and what you already know about yourself to be true. Be sure to include all aspects of yourself in your description, including your physical, social, intellectual, emotional, and spiritual sides. Add to your list whenever you notice something new about yourself. You will find that you are thinking about and looking at yourself more carefully than you ever have before. You may discover qualities about yourself that you never noticed, or you may revise a previously held notion about yourself.

Reconnect with Your Body and Your Emotions

As Marion Woodman so wisely put it: "What you know in your head will not sustain you in moments of crisis . . . confidence comes from body awareness, knowing what you feel in the moment."

The most effective way to reclaim all your emotions—pain, anger, fear, guilt, shame, joy, and love—is to begin to pay attention to your body. Even when you unconsciously repress your feelings, your body remembers them. These memories are called *body memories*. Your body remembers what it felt like when you were neglected, criticized, rejected, or smothered as a child. For each emotion, your body experiences a different set of physical sensations. It remembers with stiffness, constrictions, and tension the pain and anger you felt when you were a child.

Allow yourself to reconnect with your body, to let it express and release all the pain of childhood. Your body hurts, bleeds, tingles, or tightens for a reason. It is trying to tell you something. It is reminding you of the kinds of childhood trauma you experienced. Listen to your body and heed its messages.

One of the most effective ways of discovering who you are is to pay attention to your emotions. In fact, some define self-awareness as being conscious of our moods and our thoughts about our moods. Once again I urge you to take on a neutral stance, a nonreactive, nonjudgmental stance when observing your emotions. It helps to take a slight step back from your experience so that you can be aware of what you are feeling rather than be immersed in it.

According to Daniel Goleman in his groundbreaking book *Emotional Intelligence: Why It Can Matter More Than IQ*, "Self-awareness—recognizing a feeling as it happens—is the keystone of emotional intelligence . . . the ability to monitor feelings from moment to moment is crucial to psychological insight and understanding. . . . People with greater certainty about their feelings are better pilots of their lives, having a surer sense of how they really feel about personal decisions."

Unfortunately, for many who have been neglected and abused in childhood, emotions are a frightening thing. It was when their parents' emotions got out of hand that they got yelled at, pushed around, or hit. It was when they themselves got angry or started to cry that they were ridiculed, punished, or abandoned. For this reason, most survivors of abuse and neglect tend to deny and repress their true emotions. Even the ones who may appear to be extremely emotional, eruptive, or volatile are usually denying their more vulnerable feelings underneath.

In addition, if you were neglected or abused in childhood, you will tend to be overwhelmed and controlled by your emotions. Many people are so overwhelmed that their emotions become their enemies. Dysfunctional behaviors, including abusive or victimlike patterns, substance abuse, and suicidal tendencies, are often attempts to cope with intolerably painful emotions. Many try to regulate their emotions by trying to make themselves not feel whatever it is that they feel. This style is a direct result of the emotionally invalidating environment they were raised in, which mandated that people should smile when they are unhappy, be nice and not rock the boat when they are angry, and confess or beg for forgiveness even when they don't feel they did anything wrong.

Because of these behaviors, you may have ended up feeling sideswiped by your own emotions, or overwhelmed when your emotions build up. This, in turn, may cause you to project your feelings onto others.

What is referred to as "psychic numbing" (stuck or frozen feelings) is another frequent result of abuse and neglect in childhood. Children shut off their feelings or dissociate in response to a traumatic situation. It is as if their minds go somewhere else and they are disconnected from their bodies. Learning to re-experience frozen feelings takes time. But once these deadened feelings are liberated, they can help you by providing useful information so you can make rational decisions and take appropriate actions in your life. Reconnecting with feelings can provide you with strength, courage, and joy.

It is important that you stop labeling emotions as "good" or "bad" and instead see them as important messages that can educate you about yourself, your circumstances, and your environment. You will begin to see that your emotions can empower you to take better care of yourself and, in so doing, help you raise your self-esteem.

EXERCISE: YOUR FEELINGS LISTS

1. List some of the things that tend to make you angry.
2. What are some of the things that make you feel sad?
3. What makes you afraid?
4. What makes you feel guilty?
5. What makes you happy or joyous?
6. What makes you feel fulfilled or satisfied?

Identify Your Emotions

People who were neglected and abused as children tend to have difficulty identifying what emotion they are experiencing at any given time. This is because they may have needed to shut off their feelings in order to survive childhood trauma or neglect, or they may have had to pretend to feel something they didn't really feel. But it is also because many believed it was not safe for anyone to know what they were feeling, and as a result, they became adults with a jumble of feelings they now have difficulty identifying.

In the course of just one day we all experience myriad emotions, and learning to identify each and every one of them can be a daunting task. Therefore, it is best to focus on only a few primary emotions, at least in the beginning. According to most experts, there are eight or so primary or basic emotions: anger, sorrow, joy, surprise, fear, disgust, guilt/shame, and interest (some also consider love a primary emotion). These are considered primary emotions because we are born with the potential or biological readiness for them. All other emotions are considered secondary or social emotions because they are learned, and are usually some combination of the basic emotions. For our purposes we are going to focus on five of the primary emotions: fear, sorrow (or sadness), anger, guilt/shame, and joy.

We often become disconnected from our primary emotions by diluting them and giving them other names. For example, instead of saying they are afraid, many people will say they feel anxious or worried. Instead of saying they feel sad (or even knowing they are sad), many people will say they feel tired. And instead of saying they are angry, many people will say they are uninterested or bored.

To make it more confusing, many other words are commonly used to describe our primary emotions. The following is a list of words often used to describe the emotion of sadness. Some words describe a mild form and others more intense forms of sadness. For the most part, the list is, in order of intensity: unhappiness, hurt, dismay, melancholy, gloom, grief, sorrow, suffering, misery, despair, depression, agony, anguish, hopelessness. Sometimes using one of these words instead of the word *sad* is beneficial, because it clarifies exactly what level of sadness you are feeling. For example, agony and hopelessness certainly describe a more intense state of sadness than does *sad*. The important thing is that you not allow the description of your state to take you away from the fact that you are basically feeling the emotion of sadness.

There are also words that are closely related to the emotion of sadness, although they mean more than what we commonly identify as sadness. These include: alienation, defeat, dejection, disappointment, discontent, displeasure, distress, insecurity, isolation, neglect, pity, and rejection.

You'll notice that these words add an additional tone, judgment value, or meaning to the word *sadness*. Once again, while these words can help to describe a specific reason for your feeling of sadness, they still describe the primary emotion of sadness.

EXERCISE: THE WORDS AND FEELINGS OF SADNESS

1. Study the list of words describing the emotion of sadness. Notice how often you use these descriptive words and remind yourself that no matter what words you use, you are still feeling the primary emotion of sadness.

2. Write about the associations you have with the feeling of sadness. For example, is it okay for you to feel sadness, or do you feel it is socially unacceptable? Was it acceptable to feel sadness in your home when you were growing up? Who do you remember feeling sad when you were growing up?

How Do You Know When You Are Feeling a Particular Emotion?

The best way to discover how you are feeling is to begin by asking yourself which of the eight or nine primary feelings you are experiencing (anger, sorrow, joy, surprise, fear, disgust, guilt/shame, interest, or love). It is safe to say that at any given time we are all experiencing at least one or more of the primary emotions.

Just asking yourself the question won't necessarily help if you aren't in touch with your body. Your body is your best barometer to tell you which emotion you are feeling at any given time. Emotions involve body changes, such as fluctuations in heart rate and skin temperature and the tensing or relaxing of muscles. The most important changes are in the facial muscles. Researchers now think that changes in these muscles play an important role in actually causing emotions.

We tend to feel sadness all over our bodies in the following ways: frowning, mouth down, and eyes drooping; a slumped posture; speaking in a low, quiet, slow, or monotonous voice; heaviness in the chest, tightness in the throat, or difficulty swallowing (from holding back tears); moist eyes or tears, whimpering, crying, feeling as if you can't stop crying, or feeling that if you ever start crying you will never stop; feeling tired, run-down, or low in energy; feeling lethargic and listless, wanting to stay in bed all day; feeling as if nothing is pleasurable any more; feeling a pain or hollowness in your chest or gut; feeling empty.

Conversely, joy is usually manifested in the body in the following ways: smiling; feeling excited; feeling physically energetic, active, and "alive", feeling like laughing or giggling; having a warm glow about you; feeling "open-hearted" and loving.

You can also determine what particular emotion you are feeling by observing your behavior. The following behaviors are all indicative of someone who is feeling sad: talking about sad things; sitting or lying around; being inactive; making slow, shuffling movements; giving up and no longer trying to improve; moping, brooding, or acting moody; withdrawing from social contact; talking little or not at all.

Someone who is feeling joyous may exhibit any of the following behaviors: smiling, grinning, laughing, being bouncy or bubbly, being affectionate toward others, jumping up and down, using an enthusiastic or excited voice, talking a lot.

Emotions also involve action urges. An important function of emotions is to prompt behavior (fight in anger, flight in fear). Although the action itself is usually not considered part of the emotion, the urge to act is.

No Negative Emotions

Many people consider emotions such as fear, anger, sadness, guilt, and shame as negative. But there are no negative emotions if you view all emotions as signals or messengers telling us that something important is occurring.

What makes an emotion negative is the way we deal with it and the interpretation we give to it. For example, most people deal with these emotions in one of four negative ways:

1. They try to avoid feeling the emotion entirely (suppression).
2. They try to deny the feeling by pretending that it is not that bad (minimizing).
3. They blame someone else for making them feel as they do.
4. They deny their feeling by projecting them onto someone else.

All four of these methods prevent you from heeding the signal that the emotion is sending, from learning from the emotion, and from utilizing that knowledge to your best advantage. Even more important, when we try to avoid feeling an emotion, we deny an important part of ourselves and we risk losing touch with who we are.

Learning about Yourself through Your Emotions

The key to learning about yourself through your emotions is to experience them without inhibiting, judging, or avoiding them by distracting yourself. This is called being mindful. Instead of fighting our emotions or walling them off, being mindful of them can help us discover more about who we are. The following steps will help you to experience your emotions in a mindful way:

- Begin by simply observing your emotion. Notice how it makes you feel. Notice what happens in your body as you feel the emotion.
- Do not judge the emotion as good or bad.
- Fully experience your emotion. Allow yourself to feel it as a wave, coming and going. Try not to suppress the feelings or push the emotion away. On the other hand, don't hold onto the emotion or amplify it. Just let it pass through you like a wave.

Why It Is Important Not to Judge Our Emotions

Whenever we judge our emotions as being bad, the natural consequence is to feel guilt, shame, anxiety, and/or anger. The addition of these secondary feelings simply makes the distress more intense and intolerable. Often you will find that you can tolerate a distressing situation or painful feeling a lot better if you refrain from feeling guilty or anxious about feeling the painful emotion in the first place. Think of some occasions when you have had a secondary emotional reaction to a primary emotion, such as getting angry or feeling ashamed for getting angry, or getting depressed about being depressed. Which causes you more pain or trouble—the primary or the secondary emotion?

The following list explains how to observe an emotion nonjudgmentally:

1. Simply observe the emotion—where you feel it in your body, what sensations it elicits—without any kind of judgment or evaluation whatsoever. Refrain from labeling it "good" or "bad," "pleasant," or "painful."

2. Notice the thoughts that go through your mind as you feel this emotion, and the associations you have with it. Acknowledge the helpful, or healthy, but do not judge it. Acknowledge the harmful, or unhealthy, but do not judge it.

3. Notice the opinions you have about this feeling and about the fact that you are feeling it. Let go of your opinions and simply feel.

4. When you find yourself judging, don't judge your judging. Just stop and move on.

Being Aware of Your Emotions Can Help You to Change Them

Although there is a distinction between being aware of your feelings and acting to change them, you will find that the two actually go hand-in-hand; when you begin to recognize what you are feeling at any given time, you will be more willing and able to change that feeling.

John Mayer, a University of New Hampshire psychologist and coformulator of the theory of emotional intelligence, found that people tend to fall into distinctive styles for attending to and dealing with their emotions:

- *Self-aware.* These people are aware of their moods as they are having them. Their clarity of emotions may, in fact, be the underpinning of other personality traits they possess such as autonomy, a sureness of their own boundaries, good psychological health, and a tendency to have a positive outlook on life. When they get into a bad mood, they do not ruminate and obsess about it, and they are able to get out of it sooner than other types. In short, their mindfulness helps them manage their emotions.

- *Engulfed.* These people are often overwhelmed by their emotions and feel helpless to escape them. It is as if their moods have taken charge of them. They are not very aware of their feelings, and at the same time they tend to be rather mercurial (up and down). They become lost in their feelings rather than having some perspective. Because they feel they have no control over their emotions, they do little to try to escape bad moods.

- *Accepting.* While these people are often clear about what they are feeling, they also tend to be accepting of their moods—they don't try to change them. There are two variations of the accepting type: people who are usually in good moods and therefore have little motivation to change them, and people who are susceptible to bad moods but accept them anyway and have clarity about them. They do nothing to change their mood, no matter how negative or distressful. This pattern of behavior is often found in depressed people who are resigned to their despair.

Fill Up Your Emptiness with Your Own Feelings

Because of your low self-esteem, you, like many other survivors of emotional abuse or deprivation, have probably searched for something outside yourself for a sense of completion and a sense of being worthwhile. You may have looked to romantic love as a solution for your feelings of incompleteness and inadequacy. But no one but yourself can complete you, fill up your emptiness, or give you a sense of meaning.

If you give yourself the time and space to get to know yourself and your feelings, you will find that you can fill up the emptiness, a layer at a time. Each time you allow yourself to feel a feeling, each time you allow yourself to express an emotion, you are filling up another empty space inside.

Discover Your Essence

In addition to discovering who you are on a physical, emotional level, you need to discover that there is another aspect of you that is not related to your physical characteristics and not defined by your emotional qualities or personality type. It is the experience of who you are that is not a result of your history and conditioning and is not affected by your beliefs or opinions. This aspect of you is sometimes referred to as your *true nature*, your *being*, or your *essence*, because it is the ultimate nature of who you are. *Essence* also refers to the part of you that is most permanent and unchanging—the part of you that is central in defining who you are.

Generally speaking, we consider our bodies, our personal histories, and our emotional makeups to be the most distinctive and unchanging aspects of ourselves, the ones that define us and distinguish us from others. But in reality, they are only part of who we are. They only define our outer layer.

The negative messages you received from your parents (spoken and unspoken) became an *overlay* on top of your essence, often hiding it from your awareness. In order to reconnect with your essence, you may need to go beneath the negative parental messages you received, beneath the inner critic, and beneath your own self-judgment.

This is how Byron Brown, the author of the wonderful book *Soul without Shame: A Guide to Liberating Yourself from the Judge Within*, defines essence:

> The soul's true nature exists most fundamentally as a nowness; it is a nature that does not depend on the past or the future, nor does it depend on the experience of being a physical body. The more you have a sense of yourself as soul, the more you are aware that who you truly are is not really defined by your body. Neither is it defined by what you have learned or known in the past. Who you are is something much more intimate and immediate and something much more mysterious and harder to define. To be aware of this is to begin to open to the true nature of the soul, your own beingness *now* in your life.

According to Brown, essence (or true nature) manifests itself uniquely in every person, and that uniqueness is inherent in who you are at birth. It is not achieved, nor can it be destroyed. It is not dependent on your appearance or anything you do or accomplish. You can, however, lose touch with your true nature—or even forget that it exists. Unfortunately, this is true for many of you reading this book.

The belief in the existence of essence means you believe you have qualities or capabilities beyond those learned or instilled in you by your parents and other caretakers. As Brown states in his book, although many spiritual teachings espouse the concept of the soul's essence—that as human beings we do not begin life as a blank slate or a lump of clay ready to be shaped by our upbringing—you do not need to believe in the concept in order to benefit from this information and from connecting with your essence.

Your essence or true nature is made up of what are called *essential qualities*—attributes essential to what is most true in the experience of being human. These qualities include honesty, joy, compassion, will, strength, awareness, and peace, to name a few. Essential qualities lie deeper than habit, preference, and early conditioning, and they always exist as potentials buried in the unconscious depths of each person.

The ultimate value of who you are is based not on your attributes—your physical appearance, your IQ, your talents, or your financial success—but on the miraculous fact that you exist and that at your core you are essentially good, wise, and strong.

EXERCISE: HONORING YOUR ESSENTIAL SELF

1. Find a space inside yourself that symbolizes your internal goodness, wisdom, and strength. Using your internal voice, say your own name. Fill up the whole space with your name. Pronounce your name boldly and lovingly, and imagine that your name signifies the importance of your existence. Know that there is only one you, that there is no one else like you, that you are unique.

2. Fill your chest with your name so that you begin to feel alive inside. Remind yourself that you are a precious person, as everyone is precious.

Although we all need validation from others, the true source of your self-esteem and your power comes from within. In order to access your power, you need to stay connected with yourself. You need to develop the habit of going inside and connecting to your inherent strength, goodness, and wisdom. Doing this throughout the day, every day, will not only help you raise your self-esteem but will also help you to feel more inner strength and security.

Shedding Your Idealized Self-Image and Embracing Who You Really Are

As a child we learned what was required from us in order to be liked and accepted by our parents. The result was that we become fixated on an ideal but distorted sense of ourselves. This "ideal self" becomes an internal image of how we believe we should be so that everything will turn out all right and we will be loved, accepted, and appreciated. This ideal self-image includes personal standards for action, thought, feeling, behavior, appearance, and accomplishment.

The biggest difficulty with pursuing our ideal self-image is that it doesn't work. Although striving for the ideal as a child may have brought you parental approval, it did little to give you inner peace. The strain of constantly comparing yourself to the ideal is anxiety pro-voking and exhausting. Because it is impossible to reach an ideal, we are bound to fail and we always find ourselves lacking, deficient, or not good enough. This sets us up for more shame and guilt. Even though the ideal may be worthy, at some point we need to question just how good it is when we use it as a way to continually reject ourselves.

Psychological Truths of the Week

- Those who were emotionally abused or neglected as children often do not develop a clear, undistorted image of themselves. By creating a Mirror Journal and a self-portrait, and by completing various other activities, survivors can gain a clearer image of themselves—their likes, dislikes, values, goals, and dreams.

- Parents project their own unresolved issues onto their children. In order to heal from the damage this causes, adult children need to reject the distorted mirror their parents put on them and create a new mirror that reflects more accurately who they actually are.

- Those who were emotionally abused or neglected as children tend to either become numb to their emotions, feel sideswiped by them, or feel overwhelmed when their emotions build up.

Mirror Therapy Assignment #8: Accepting and Embracing Your Less-Than-Ideal Self

1. Refer back to the description of yourself and the list you made earlier in this chapter. Go through your description and make two lists, the first being all your positive qualities, abilities, talents, and areas of growth. The other list will include negative qualities, traits, limits, and bad habits.

2. Now read over your list of positive qualities and really take them in. Allow yourself to feel the pride that comes from acknowledging that you do, in fact, possess these good qualities.

3. Read over your list of negative or less-than-perfect quali-ties. Try to be neutral and simply acknowledge these aspects of yourself without becoming critical of yourself. For example, say, "It is true that I tend to be impatient and critical and that I lack very much athletic ability."

4. Decide which of your less-than-perfect qualities you wish to work on and which ones you need to simply accept. For example, "I wish I was not so impatient and critical, and I am working on it. As far as my lack of athletic ability, I think I just need to accept that I will never be a jock."

5. Take still another look at your list of your best attributes (your sense of humor, your intelligence, your generosity,

your courage, your strong legs, your shiny hair, your smile, your ability to dance, your ability to empathize with others). Now read this list out loud. Notice how you feel when you read the list. If you feel shy about your positive attributes, try reading the list louder, with a stronger voice. Feel pride as you read about what a great person you are!

6. Pick out two or three items that you would like to reinforce in yourself. Make a concerted effort to acknowledge these traits and/or to reinforce these behaviors whenever you can. Praising or rewarding yourself each time you become aware of these traits or behaviors will help to raise your self-esteem.

9

Providing for Yourself What You Missed as a Child

*The curious paradox is that when I accept myself
just as I am, then I can change.*

—CARL ROGERS

*Self-nurturing means, above all, making a
commitment to self-compassion.*

—JENNIFER LOUDEN, *The Woman's Comfort Book*

*The feeling of being valuable—"I am a valuable person" is
essential to mental health and is a cornerstone of self-discipline . . .
because when one considers oneself valuable one will take care of
oneself in all ways that are necessary. Self-discipline is self-caring."*

—M. SCOTT PECK, *The Road Less Traveled*

IN THIS CHAPTER WE ARE GOING to focus on helping you to provide for yourself many of the things you missed out on as a child—namely, empathetic mirroring and nurturing and responsive parenting.

To grow up to be a whole person, infants, toddlers, and children in their formative years need the experience of genuine acceptance. They have to know they are truly seen and yet are perfect and lovable in their parents' eyes. They need to stumble and sometimes fall and to be greeted by a father's or a mother's sympathetic concern. Through parental acceptance, children learn that their essential selves merit love. In other words, when the mirror we gazed into is clear and undistorted, we see ourselves as we truly are. Unfortunately, children raised by overly critical, narcissistic, or demanding parents have their essential self rejected by their parents.

In an ideal world, our parents or primary caretakers were genuinely concerned about us when we were hurt. They tended to our wounds and spoke to us in a loving tone, and they let us know through their words and actions that they understood what we were experiencing— thus providing an accurate mirror. We felt accepted and understood.

When a child is treated with empathy, that is, when parents accurately understand and sensitively respond to the child's thoughts and feelings, she learns that she is worthy of love and is worthwhile. The child's empathy and compassion for herself increases by leaps and bounds as she mirrors what the outside world has revealed to her about her self-worth. If, on the other hand, a child is not given this empathetic mirroring, she doesn't feel loved and is not able to feel compassion toward herself. In this chapter you will learn how to love and accept yourself as you really are and to provide this positive, empathetic mirroring for yourself.

Children also need a combination of what Laurel Mellin, the creator of the Solutions Program and *The Pathway*, calls a "nurturing, responsive internal mother" and a "safe, powerful, internal father." In this chapter you will also learn how to become your own nurturing mother and limit-setting father. Equally important, you will learn how to soothe yourself in healthy ways.

How to Provide Empathetic Mirroring for Yourself

Elan Golumb, the author of *Trapped in the Mirror: Adult Children of Narcissists in Their Struggle for Self*, writes about the importance of what she refers to as "the rounded eye": "All children need the beneficial glance of what I call the rounded eye, one that does not focus on and evaluate parts of our being. The rounded eye looks on all unconditionally. It gives us acceptance and heals the damage of our upbringing."

If you were emotionally abused, you were likely raised under your parents' ignoring or scrutinizing gaze. Growing up under such a regime, you may have felt at times as if you were a bug under a microscope. At other times you may have felt like a child abandoned in a corner. As a result you may have internalized the quest for your flaws and begun to watch yourself in a critical and rejecting way. Your parents' scrutiny turned your spontaneity into paralysis. Instead of feeling free to explore the world and to discover the things you loved to do, you learned to constrict yourself in order to get away from parental criticism. In order to counter these tendencies and correct your distorted self-image, you need to work on accepting yourself just the way you are.

Looking at yourself with a rounded eye is looking with compassion instead of constantly judging yourself. Here are some suggestions to help you trade in your critical eye for a compassionate one:

- Whenever you make a mistake or fail to reach a particular goal, instead of letting your inner critic take over and chastise you mercilessly, tell yourself, "I did the best I could" or, "I'm only human and humans make mistakes." This is not the same as making excuses for your behavior; it is just a compassionate acknowledgment that we can all fail, even when we try our hardest. You will be far more motivated to try harder the next time if you talk to yourself in a kind, understanding way than if you tear down your self-esteem.

- Whenever you make a mistake or fail to reach a particular goal, remind yourself that your value is not dependent on your achievements. Remind yourself that you have inherent value and worth—your essential self.

- Whenever you fail to reach a goal, ask yourself whether your goal was a reasonable one. Did you set your sights too high, considering who you are today and your present circumstances? Often we set goals or have expectations of ourselves that are not reasonable. Begin to set more reasonable expectations for yourself. Instead of setting goals that are impossible to reach, set goals that are possible and will give your self-esteem a boost when you reach them.

Creating a Nurturing Inner Voice (Mothering)

One of the primary ways of providing positive empathetic mirroring for yourself is by creating an internal nurturing voice. Creating a nurturing inner voice can help to soften and balance the negative introject. It is like giving to ourselves the responsive parent that so many of us did not have.

How do you create a nurturing inner voice? How do you substitute a more positive, responsive voice to take the place of the internalized critical voice of your parents? Just as you need to plant seeds or bulbs in order to get a garden, you need to plant a nurturing voice in yourself.

1. Begin by going inside yourself and consciously creating an intimate connection with yourself. Many people don't know how to do this. Others are afraid to do it because their inner life seems like a cold, uninviting place. You can start by simply asking yourself, "How do I feel?" as many times a day as you can think of it. You may need to prompt yourself to go inside by leaving yourself written reminders like "Check in with yourself" or "How are you feeling?"

2. Bring up a nurturing but strong inner voice, one that is deeply connected to the inherent strength, goodness, and wisdom within you (your essence). Some people are readily able to find such a voice, while others have more difficulty. If you find that it is difficult to find a nurturing voice, adopt the voice of someone you know who is nurturing but strong (your therapist, a sponsor, a loving friend).

3. Whenever you find you are criticizing yourself or being hard on yourself, consciously switch to this more nurturing voice. This is especially important for people who were highly criticized by

a parent. They need to replace their parent's critical, negative voice with a more nurturing, compassionate inner voice.

4. Make it a practice to regularly give yourself credit for the progress you have made or for the good things you have done.

If You Are Having Difficulty Creating a Nurturing Voice

You met Lorraine earlier in the book. Her mother was never pleased with anything she did. When Lorraine grew up, she unfortunately took on her mother's critical stance. Her mother's harsh voice echoed within her. When I started working with Lorraine, I asked her to begin to pay attention to the critical voice inside and to begin to replace it with a nurturing inner voice. But Lorraine was having a lot of difficulty doing this. "I can't find a nurturing voice. I only hear my mother's." Later on she told me that on occasion she heard my voice. "Sometimes I'll wonder whether I should do something and I'll hear your voice asking me whether doing this would be taking care of myself. Other times I hear you talking to me in a soft way, the way you do when you know I'm really hurting." Lorraine had used my voice as her nurturing voice until she could develop her own. It is perfectly acceptable to use the voice of someone else who makes you feel loved, cared for, and accepted. You may also try using the voice that you use when you are talking to a child or a pet. Recent studies show that a sweet, high-pitched voice is the one babies respond to the most.

Become Your Own Nurturing Parent

In addition to creating a nurturing inner voice, you also need to provide for yourself the nurturing and responsiveness you missed as a child. Begin by writing about what you learned about nurturing and responsiveness as a child.

WRITING EXERCISE: YOUR NURTURING HISTORY

1. Think about how your parents met their own needs. Do you think your parents were connected to how they felt emotionally and what their true needs were? Write about

how you observed your parents taking care of themselves or nurturing themselves.

2. Think about how your parents took care of your needs. Did your parents treat you as if you had a right to have your needs met? Did you get the sense that your feelings mattered to them? Write about whether you felt your parents were responsive, depriving, or indulgent toward you.

3. Think about whether your parents taught you how to nurture yourself. Did your parents talk to you about how to take care of yourself? Did they talk to you about honoring your feelings and needs? Did they teach you how to soothe and comfort yourself?

4. Think about the ways you have nurtured yourself as an adult. Do you know how you feel and what you need at any given time? Are you able to soothe and comfort yourself from within? Do you tend to either indulge yourself or deprive yourself instead of being responsive toward yourself?

Your Need for Structure (Fathering)

As important as it is to create a nurturing inner voice (symbolic of a healthy mother), it is equally important to provide yourself with healthy limits (symbolic of a strong father). While mothers represent nurturing, fathers represent safety, structure, and limits. Historically, mothers have primarily been responsible for providing nurturing to their children, and it has been the role of the father to provide discipline (thus the "just wait until your father comes home" message given by many mothers).

If your parents were not able or willing to nurture you properly, they probably weren't very good at setting limits either. Without clear limits and expectations, you may feel confused, lost, powerless, or unsafe. It has been found that children who do not receive proper limits and moral guidance tend to become either impulsive and aggressive or fearful and passive.

Questionnaire: Your Limits

1. Did your parents have reasonable expectations of you— neither too harsh nor too easy?

2. Were their expectations communicated to you clearly, or was it a constant guessing game of trying to figure out what their expectations were?

3. Did your parents tend to refrain from either depriving you or indulging you?

4. Were your parents good role models concerning setting personal limits with themselves?

5. Did you frequently witness one or both of your parents going overboard when it came to eating, drinking alcohol, working too hard, shopping, or any other excess?

6. Did you frequently witness one or both of your parents depriving herself or himself of proper nutrition, adequate rest or sleep, or recreation?

7. Did your parents ever talk to you about setting limits on yourself?

8. Did your parents talk to you about having reasonable expectations of yourself?

9. Do you have reasonable expectations for yourself today?

10. Do you tend to avoid depriving yourself or indulging yourself?

If your parents were unable to set healthy limits on your behavior, you will tend to either be too easy or too hard on yourself. You may be so harsh with yourself, expecting so much, that there is little room in your life for pleasure. Or the reverse may be true and you may be so easy on yourself that you let yourself or others down. You may have become perfectionistic, pushing yourself beyond normal human limits and driving yourself mercilessly. Or you may do the opposite and hesitate to take action, procrastinate whenever you have a task to do, or tend to abandon projects instead of following through.

So how do you create a strong, limit-setting internal father? How do you begin providing healthy limits for yourself?

In order to set effective limits with a child, a parent must observe him and get to know him intimately. She must be able to determine when the child needs direction and when he needs room to learn his own lessons. She must be able to decide when a child needs to be told "no" and when he needs to be given a little slack. You will need to do the same for yourself. This means you will need to consistently pay attention to yourself by monitoring your emotions and observing your behavior in order to discover when you need to set limits on yourself. In other words, you need to pay attention to yourself in order to know when you need to hear a nurturing voice and when you need to hear a limit-setting voice. Otherwise, you will be too hard on yourself when you really need encouragement or too easy on yourself when you need to provide some limits or structure.

For example, if you tend to stay up too late at night and then feel exhausted in the morning, you are not setting appropriate limits for yourself. So how do you go about changing this? The first step is to notice the behavior and consequences of the behavior. Make a notation in your Mirror Journal about how you feel in the morning and all through the day when you stay up too late at night.

The next step is to make a commitment to changing the behavior, even if it is only a little at a time. For example, commit to going to bed just fifteen minutes earlier for one week. The next week, commit to going to bed another fifteen minutes earlier. In your journal, note any improvements in your energy level or attitude that you might notice with each fifteen-minute change. Continue this process until you have changed your bedtime to something that is reasonable and healthy for you.

It can be very difficult to get the concept that setting limits on one-self can be a loving and nurturing thing to do. This is particularly true when limits always felt like deprivation, or when parents set limits as punishment. But as the quote by M. Scott Peck at the beginning of the chapter stated, "Self-discipline is self-caring." Another way of saying this is: "Limit-setting equals love." If you can consistently remind yourself of this, it will help you overcome your resistance to limit-setting. If you continue to have difficulties learning how to set limits for yourself, especially if you have addiction problems such as compulsive overeating or alcohol abuse, I strongly recommend the Solutions Program created by Laurel Mellin. For more information on the program, refer to "Recommended Therapies" in the appendix.

Another way of working on setting limits with yourself is by doing inner-child work. Refer to chapter 11 for more information on this.

The setting of reasonable expectations for yourself, which was discussed earlier, is another important aspect of creating a strong internal father. The Solutions Program will also help you learn to set reasonable expectations of yourself. If you don't have reasonable expectations of yourself, which are neither too harsh nor too lenient, either you will set yourself up to feel disappointed in yourself (and activate your critical inner voice), or you will not take action that will allow you to reach your true potential.

A reasonable expectation is reachable, given your history, your present situation, and who you are today. For example, it is *reasonable* that given your history of being emotionally abused, you may suffer from low self-esteem, a strong inner critic, and some unhealthy shame. It is *unreasonable* to expect that given your history, you would be able to overcome the negative effects of emotional abuse overnight. It is *reasonable*, however, to expect that by reading this book and doing the exercises, you may be able to overcome much of the damage you suffered.

Exercise: Your Expectations of Yourself

- Make a list of the expectations or goals you have for yourself.
- Review this list and determine which of these expectations seems reasonable (meaning that you are capable of meeting these expectations, given who you are today and your present circumstances).

Creating Balance in Your Life

Even the most well-meaning parents tend to lack a sense of balance when it comes to their parenting style. They either tend to be depriving or permissive. The cause of these parenting styles can be traced back to the parents' own upbringing (for example, their parents were overly smothering and "merged" with their child, or their parents were overly removed and "disengaged"). As Laurel Mellin states in her book *The Pathway: Follow the Road to Health and Happiness*, "These patterns are etched into the feeling brain early in life, then tend to be passed along from one generation to the next."

Deprivation and permissiveness are actually two sides of the same coin. Parents who were deprived themselves when they were children will tend to either deprive their own children or become overly indulgent toward their children in their determination not to make their parents' mistakes.

Becoming Your Own Responsive Parent

As Laurel Mellin explains in her program, the goal is to create a balance between the two extremes—being neither depriving nor indulgent toward oneself. This middle point is called "responsiveness." A responsive parent is keenly aware of her child's needs. She is attentive to her child and has a desire to meet her needs once she discovers what they are. She doesn't change her baby's diapers when the baby is crying because it is hungry. Neither does she try to feed her baby when what the child really needs is to be held. When a responsive parent discovers and fulfills her child's real need, she doesn't need to indulge the child to make up for any neglectful treatment on her part. She knows she has been responsive to her child's real needs and doesn't suffer from feelings of guilt.

Just as a responsive parent is aware of her child's needs, we need to become aware of and sensitive to our own needs. Once we have identified our real needs we are better able to meet them. Unfortunately, discovering our real needs is not usually that easy, especially if we had depriving or overly permissive parents.

How Do I Know What I Need?

Adults who were neglected or emotionally abused often do not know how to take care of themselves. Because their needs were often ignored by their parents, adult survivors often continue to ignore them.

EXERCISE: OUR BASIC NEEDS

Take a close look at the following list of basic needs and think about how often you provide them for yourself:

- Hunger—Give yourself healthy food to eat.
- Thirst—Give yourself plenty of water, not diet colas or sweet drinks.
- Sleep—Go to bed at a reasonable time; don't eat before bed or take any stimulants.
- Companionship—Don't allow yourself to stay isolated; reach out when you are lonely.
- Sex—Provide yourself with healthy outlets for sex, neither depriving nor indulging yourself.
- Stimulation—Get involved in activities that stimulate your mind, body, and spirit.
- Spiritual connection—Satisfy your need for contemplation, gratitude, prayer, ritual, or any other type of spiritual expression you need.

The Connection between Needs and Feelings

One way of discovering what your needs are at any given time is to check in with your feelings. They will tell you what you need if you pay close attention. The following exercise, based on a process by Laurel Mellin in her Solutions Program, will help you make this important connection (see the appendix at the back of this book).

EXERCISE: FEELINGS AND NEEDS

1. Check in with yourself several times a day by going inside and asking yourself what you are feeling.
2. When you find a feeling, look for the corresponding need. Ask yourself, "What do I need?" Often the answer will be

"feel my feeling and let it fade." Answer in the simplest way instead of confusing the issue with too many details or complexities. For example, if you are hungry, you need food. When you feel guilty, you need to apologize.

3. It may take trying on several needs before you find the one that is true for you. You may also have many needs attached to one feeling. For example, you may feel *lonely* and your *need* may be to call a friend, to get a hug from your partner, or to connect with yourself.

4. Be on the alert for answers that are not truly responsive to you. For example, "I feel sad"; "I need some candy"; "I feel angry"; "I need to hit him." Tap into your inherent wisdom and relax into a more logical, self-nurturing answer. Ask yourself, "Okay, what do I really need?" For example, "to express myself (write, sing)," "to get physical (walk, stomp)," "to develop a plan," "to learn from it (next time I will . . .)."

A Self-Care Assessment

The following questions refer to your ability to *self-nurture* and *set limits*. Write "true" or "false" next to each item:

1. I am aware of what I am feeling at any given time.
2. I am numb to my feelings a great deal of the time.
3. I am able to recognize and meet my needs.
4. I am not able to recognize my needs so I cannot meet them.
5. I am able to ask for help from others.
6. I remain isolated from others and cannot ask for help.
7. I am able to set reasonable expectations (neither too harsh nor too easy).
8. The expectations I set for myself are often either too harsh or too easy.
9. I am aware of a safe place inside me.
10. I feel empty, numb, or lost a great deal of the time.
11. My inner voice is nurturing and warm.

12. My inner voice is critical and demanding.
13. When life is hard, I soothe myself from within.
14. When life is hard, I soothe myself with food, alcohol, drugs, or other external solutions.
15. I can feel the pain of the past and let it go.
16. I shut out my bad feelings about the past.
17. I am physically active.
18. I am not physically active.
19. I eat a healthy diet.
20. I do not eat a healthy diet.
21. I take time to restore my body, mind, and spirit.
22. I continue to push myself to do, do, do.

If your answers were mostly "false" to the odd-numbered questions and mostly "true" to the even-numbered questions, you are not able to self-nurture or set limits very well. Because survivors of emotional abuse or neglect are often disconnected or numb to their feelings, you probably do not know what your needs actually are at any given time. You may not feed yourself when your body needs fuel, because you are numb to the feelings of hunger. You may not allow yourself to cry or to seek out someone to talk to, because you do not know when you are feeling sad or lonely.

If your basic need for nurturing, limits, protection, and support were not met by neglectful or self-absorbed parents, you will have a difficult time knowing how to meet those needs now. It is as if there is a disconnect inside you between what you need and providing it for yourself. A child needs to receive love in order to be able to feel love. This includes love for oneself. If we do not love ourselves, we will not be motivated to take care of ourselves. Those of us who were neglected or emotionally abused often look with wonder at others who are motivated to take care of themselves. "Where do they get the motivation?" we ask ourselves. "Why do they care so much about their health or the way they look?" We are poignantly aware that there is something missing in us, something that creates the kind of motivation that would cause someone to say no to a piece of cake, the kind of motivation to get up at six o'clock in the morning in order to get to the gym before going to work, the kind of motivation that would help someone leave an abusive partner. The something that is missing is self-love.

Others care for their bodies but do not care for their emotions or their souls. They can spend hours working out at the gym but not even five minutes checking in with how they feel. They can spend the weekend running, biking, or climbing and not spend a moment alone connecting to their soul. Or they devote so much time to worrying about how they look on the outside that they lose track of who they are on the inside.

Some adults who were neglected or emotionally abused do not take care of themselves because they do not feel they deserve it. Children tend to blame the neglect and abuse they experience on themselves, in essence saying to themselves, "My mother is treating me like this because I've been bad" or "I am being neglected because I am unlovable." Adult survivors tend to continue this kind of rationalization, believing that they are to blame for their own deprivation and abuse as a child. As adults they put up with poor treatment by friends, relatives, and romantic partners because they believe they brought it on themselves. When good things happen to them, they may actually become uncomfortable. They feel so unworthy that they cannot take the good in.

Exercise: Why Do You Not Take Better Care of Yourself?

- Write down the reasons why you believe you do not take care of yourself better.
- List all the ways that you deprive yourself of nurturing, support, protection, and so forth.

Learning How to Soothe Yourself in Healthy Ways

Another aspect of self-care is the ability to soothe yourself. A responsive mother reacts quickly to her child's cries. She picks up her baby and soothes her with a gentle voice and touch. She ascertains what her baby needs, whether it is food, a diaper change, or simply to be held and comforted. This is considered an empathetic response, which makes the baby feel safe and reassured. From experiences like this, infants learn in a deeply unconscious way that they can get what they need, when they need it, and that all will be okay. This unconscious experience of knowing that they will be responded to adequately and that everything will be taken care of translates into an ability to *self-soothe*.

Now let's imagine another infant and another mother. This time the mother is distracted and impatient. Her baby's helplessness and the immediacy of his needs trigger her own fears and fragile sense of self. Instead of responding calmly and confidently, she acts anxious and impatient, and she communicates (nonverbally) to her baby that things are not safe. Instead of experiencing the relief of a soothing response, the baby feels even more anxious. The more distressed he becomes, the more distressed his mother becomes. Even food or a clean diaper cannot soothe him, because he is too overwhelmed by the quality of his mother's care.

If this mother consistently treats her child this way or in other less-than-nurturing ways (such as being left alone for long periods of time or receiving unpredictable responses), he is likely to grow into an adult who is unable to soothe himself effectively. He may feel off balance and distressed whenever he is in a situation that is challenging or uncertain. From these early experiences he will likely develop the expectation that things will *not* be okay, that he cannot get his needs met, and that the world is an unsafe place. Of course, some children are inherently more sensitive and more vulnerable to nonempathetic responses.

You may have noticed that when life presents challenges, you often experience an intensity of distress that feels excessive and out of control. Or you may experience a depth of hopelessness and futility that seems overwhelmingly powerful. If this is true for you, it may be because your needs were not responded to in a soothing, nurturing way when you were an infant. It may also mean that as an infant you experienced a great deal of interpersonal chaos (such as often hearing your parents fighting), parental neglect, or rage.

Even with these early experiences, you can learn to self-soothe, to calm yourself even when you aren't consciously aware that you need it. You can also learn to listen to your needs and honor them. By developing the ability to self-soothe, you also learn to love yourself even when you make mistakes and to stop ignoring your body's signals for rest and nutrition.

This ability to self-soothe begins with creating a nurturing inner voice. When you find yourself in a distressful situation, instead of allowing yourself to become overly fearful or to obsess anxiously over what could or could not happen, talk to yourself in a calm, nurturing way (you can do this silently, inside your head, or, if you are alone, you can talk out loud). Say things like "You're okay" or "You're going to get through this just fine." When you feel criticized, or when your inner critic starts to go on a tirade, soothe yourself by telling yourself that it is okay not to be perfect, that you are okay just the way you are, imperfections and all.

You can also learn to self-soothe by connecting with the child inside. Refer to chapter 11 for instructions on how to do this. Once you've learned how to connect with your inner child, you can practice listening to her needs, paying attention to her, holding her, and talking to her. By doing this on a consistent basis, you will learn how to calm yourself when you are in a distressful or insecure situation.

Treating Ourselves the Way Our Parents Treated Us

Many survivors of neglect and emotional abuse end up treating themselves exactly the way their depriving, abandoning, controlling, shaming, or self-absorbed parents treated them. You may be so used to being deprived that you continue to deprive yourself. You may be so used to being abandoned that you abandon yourself.

Exercise: How You Neglect and Deprive Yourself the Way Your Parents Did

An important aspect of self-care is discovering all the ways you treat yourself the way your parents treated you as a child.

1. Make a list of the ways you neglect or deprive yourself of what you need.

2. Write down every example you can think of regarding how your parents neglected to take care of you. Include ways they deprived you physically as well as emotionally. Also include the ways they indulged you. Here is my list:

- My mother didn't take care of my personal hygiene and didn't teach me how to do so (brush my teeth, wash and comb my hair).

- She dressed me funny when I was small and didn't teach me how to coordinate my clothes after I was old enough to dress myself.

- She had a barber cut my hair too short—it made me look like a boy.

- She didn't have fresh fruits and vegetables in the home and didn't cook vegetables.

- She didn't provide any limits regarding how much I could eat.

- She didn't get up in the morning to prepare my breakfast before I went to school and didn't have breakfast food available.

- She allowed me to stay up too late at night.

- She didn't play games with me or provide any stimulation.

- She left me alone a great deal of the time.

3. Take a close look at your list and see if there is a connection between the way you treat yourself today and the way you were treated by your parents. Now write a list of all the ways you neglect or indulge yourself. Here are my responses:

- I have a difficult time spending money on fruits and vegetables. I tell myself it is too much money and then end up buying sweets instead.

- I have a tendency to eat too much—partly out of a feeling of deprivation, a fear of not getting enough, and partly out of habit.

- I stay up too late at night.
- I have a difficult time getting up in the morning and I seldom eat breakfast.
- I tend to lead a sedentary life (read, watch TV) like my mother, and only recently got involved in swimming and biking.
- I tend to isolate myself from others (I don't call my friends or make arrangements to go places with them very often).

You do not have to stay trapped in repeating the depriving and indulging patterns you learned from your parents. Although it is tempting to indulge yourself in order to make up for what you did not receive as a child, this will not make up for the deprivation you experienced. The only thing that will begin to make up for what you did not receive as a child is for you to become the responsive, nurturing parent to yourself that you deserved all along.

Psychological Truths of the Week

- Starting in infancy, children need positive, empathetic mirroring from their parents in order to know they have worth.
- Adults who were emotionally abused or deprived as children need to create a nurturing, responsive, internal "mother" and a safe, powerful internal "father" in order to provide for themselves what they missed out on as children. This involves learning nurturing skills and learning to set effective limits.
- If childrens' needs and feelings are continually ignored or discounted they will not know how to soothe themselves.
- By committing to the process of change and growth, we can discover that when we are more accepting of ourselves—even with all our faults and flaws—we are free to become the person we were meant to be.

Mirror Therapy Assignment #9:
Making a Commitment to Begin
Meeting Your Needs

1. Think about what you wanted from your parents that you didn't receive. For example, did you want their encouragement? Their approval? Did you crave more affection? Make a list of all the things you wished you had received from your parents but did not get.

2. List the ways you plan to start meeting your needs and the things you are going to do in order to provide for yourself what your parents didn't give to you.

3. Make a commitment to begin doing one concrete action that will provide for you what you missed as a child.

10

Learning to Love Your Body

The body is a sacred garment.

—Martha Graham, *Blood Memory*

It is difficult to love your body when your parents criticized the way it looked or made you feel like it was dirty or shameful. It is even difficult to take ownership of your body when your parents treated your body as if it were their property—as if they had a right to hit you or neglect you whenever they wanted. How can you think of your body as sacred and what you put into it as important when your body's needs for adequate food, rest, or exercise were ignored? How can you feel like taking care of your body or protecting it from harm when it was regularly exposed to unhealthy conditions? In this chapter I present a number of exercises that will help you to connect with your body, learn about yourself from it, show appreciation for it, stop judging it, and ultimately, to love it.

Connecting with Your Body

Survivors of emotional abuse and neglect tend to become numb to their bodies. They tend to disown them. Because their parents ignored their needs, they continue to ignore their bodies' signals and needs. Some even treat their bodies as if they were the enemy. The following questionnaire will provide you with a better sense of how connected you are to your body.

Questionnaire: Your Relationship with Your Body

Depending on how often, if ever, the following statements are true, give yourself a score of 1 for never, 2 for sometimes, and 3 for always.

1. I have a good sense of my body.
2. On the whole, I am happy with the way my body looks.
3. I am connected with my body; I rarely split off or numb myself to my feelings.
4. I pay attention to the messages my body sends me.
5. I don't deprive myself of adequate food, water, sleep, or appropriate clothing.
6. I treat my body well by providing healthy food in moderate amounts, regular exercise, and plenty of sleep.
7. I rarely fall, trip, or bump into things.
8. I rarely push my body beyond its limits in terms of physical exertion, lack of sleep, or other deprivations.
9. I do not poison my body with excess alcohol, cigarettes, or recreational drugs.
10. I stand firmly and comfortably on both my feet.
11. I breathe regularly and deeply.
12. I hold my head up high and my shoulders back.
13. I enjoy hugging and being hugged.
14. I allow myself to laugh often and freely.
15. I regularly receive massages to help relax my body and increase my self-esteem.

Add up your responses. If your total is 37 to 45, you enjoy a wonderfully positive relationship with your body; if your total is 26 to 36, your body deserves more care and respect from you; if your total is 15 to 25, your relationship with your body needs repair.

Your body is there to support you in doing all the things you want to do. It is there to help you feel safe, protected, joyous, and childlike.

Instead of thinking of your body as an "it," a possession, or a beast to be tamed and mastered, begin to create a new relationship with your body. Allow yourself to be led by your body's strength and wisdom.

Your Body as a Teacher

Your body is a wealth of information. It holds the memory of trauma long forgotten that is nevertheless still affecting you. It can tell you how you are feeling and what you need at any particular time.

EXERCISE: LEARNING FROM YOUR BODY

1. Today, all day, pay attention to your breath. How are you breathing right now? Deeply or shallowly? Do you sometimes forget to breathe for long periods of time?

2. Identify the emotion your breath is expressing—anxiety, relaxation, irritation, fear. What can you learn from your breathing pattern? Write your answers down in your mirror journal.

3. Notice which parts of your body are the most tense. If these parts could speak, what would they say? What would they tell you they need? What would they tell you about past trauma?

4. Which parts of your body are the most numb? Why have these parts of your body lost all feeling? Underneath the numbness is probably a lot of pain; what is this pain about?

Sometimes we focus all our negativity on one part of our body. We become convinced that this part is responsible for all our bad feelings about ourselves. I mentioned an extreme version of this earlier in the book when I briefly discussed body dysmorphic disorder. People who were sexually abused often feel extremely negative about the parts of their bodies that were involved with the abuse (their breasts, their vagina, their penis). If your bad feelings about your body seem to focus on one body part, the following exercise may help.

EXERCISE: LEARNING FROM YOUR LEAST FAVORITE BODY PART

1. In your journal, write about what part of your body you like the least and why. For example, do you dislike this part of your body because others have criticized it, or does it cause you to resemble one of your parents? If you don't know the answer, complete the following sentence over and over until you come up with the reasons:

   "I dislike this part of my body because_____."

   Don't think about your answer ahead of time, just continue to complete the sentence until you have no more answers.

2. Imagine that you are having a conversation with this body part. What do you imagine it might say to you if it could speak?

3. If you having difficulty, draw a vertical line down the center of a piece of paper. On the left-hand side, ask this part of your body a question. For example, you might ask, "Is there something you want me to know?" or "Why do you look like you do?" or "Is there something you can teach me?" On the right side of the paper write the answer. Don't think about what you're going to write, just let your subconscious do it for you.

My client Tracy identified her stomach as her least-liked part of her body. When she did this exercise, she asked her stomach, "Is there something you want me to know?"

The answer came quickly, "I want you to know that I feel bloated and uncomfortable! You fed me too much yesterday and I don't like it. I feel embarrassed."

When she asked, "Is there something you can teach me? Why do you get so big?" the answer was, "I get big because you eat too much and eat the wrong food. But also because you need me to protect you. No one can get close to you if I stick out. They can't hurt you."

Tracy's mother had been extremely critical of her as she was growing up. Tracy began to find comfort in food, especially by eating starchy foods. By the time she was twelve, her stomach stuck out like a pregnant woman's. Tracy's stomach acted as a shield, keeping people away and numbing her to her own feelings.

Your Body's Story

Your body has a story to tell. There are messages in the lines of your face and the contours of your body. There are secrets hidden in your musculature.

1. Look at yourself in the mirror or at a recent picture of yourself. What do you see? Look beyond the surface appearance (and whether you look "good" or not) and see what your body says about you. Notice how you are standing. Are you erect or slouched? Do you seem uncomfortable or tense? Are you smiling or frowning? Is your hair shining and healthy or dull? Record your observations and write about what these things are saying about you.

2. Draw an outline of your body. You can use your imagination, a photo, or the mirror to get the shape and proportions.

3. Using a red pen or pencil, color in the areas of your body that are carrying pain or stress right now. You may have tight neck muscles, a headache, or an upset stomach. If you are not sure where your stress lies, start at your head and work your way down your entire body, checking in with each part to see if stress has landed there.

4. Using a blue pen or pencil, color in the areas of your body where you hold chronic stress or pain. This may be the site of a previous accident or childhood abuse (for example, you have chronic pain in your neck due to your mother's slapping you in the face so often, or you may suffer from chronic gynecological problems due to the sexual abuse you experienced).

5. Using a black pen or pencil, darken the areas of your body that you are critical of, or your parents were critical of or the parts of your body that hold a great deal of shame.

6. With a green pen or pencil, color in the areas of your body that feel relaxed and at ease.

7. Observe what this picture tells you about yourself. Is your drawing covered with red, blue, and black with only little patches of green? If this is true, you are in desperate need of self-nurturing, relaxation, and self-acceptance.

Our Parents, Our Bodies

Our parents shape not only our personalities but also the way we view and value our bodies as well. Did your parents treat your body with respect, or did they treat it as if it was a possession that they could access or intrude upon whenever they wanted? Did they like your body, or were they critical of it? Do you see any similarities between the way your parents treated your body and the way you now treat it?

EXERCISE: ARE YOU TREATING YOUR BODY THE WAY YOUR PARENTS DID?

List all the ways that you mistreat your body today. Take a close look at this list and see if you can make a connection between how your parents treated your body and how you are now treating your body. Here is my list:

- My mother allowed me to stay up too late at night so I didn't get enough sleep.

- I still stay up too late and am often sleep deprived.

- My mother didn't get up in the morning to make me breakfast.

- I don't make myself breakfast.

- My mother allowed me to eat a huge plate of food at dinner (often late at night just before bed).

- I tend to wait until late at night to eat and then am so hungry that I eat a huge plate of food just before bed.

Valuing Your Body

In addition to being disconnected from your body, you probably don't value it enough. The more you value your body, the better choices you will make concerning its care. Similarly, the more you love your body, the more likely you will be to cultivate positive health habits: eating more nutritious meals, exercising regularly, listening to your body's wisdom to inform you of what you need, treating yourself kindly when you are sick.

Exercise: Thank Your Body

The following exercise will help you begin to feel and express gratitude for your body and all it does for you.

- Express appreciation and gratitude for each part of your body. For example, thank your arms for the many things they do for you, for the incredible aspects of life you enjoy because of them: "Thank you for allowing me to hug my children," "Thank you for making it possible for me to embrace my husband," "Thank you for helping me to protect myself from assault," "Thank you for making it possible for me to carry groceries."

- Continue this process until you have acknowledged and thanked every major part of your body.

- Notice how each part of your body feels after you have expressed your gratitude.

Body Acceptance

In order to be able to value and love your body, you also need to accept it the way it is—including all your limitations, flaws, and imperfections. The following exercise will help you discover how much you accept your body today and will assist you in beginning to work toward more body acceptance.

Exercise: Body Acceptance

1. Write about how you feel about your body today. Include which parts of your body you accept and which parts you are critical of. Do you continue to take your body for granted?

2. Take some time to think about a part of your body you don't especially like. Write a letter to that body part, thanking it for remaining a part of your body in spite of your ungrateful attitude. Include an apology to it for being so critical and ungrateful.

3. Do something nice for that part of your body today. It has been putting up with a lot of criticism and ungratefulness from you. (For example, if you have been critical of your stomach, put some warm oil on it and caress it lovingly.)

Look at Yourself with New Eyes

You don't need to constantly try to meet some external notion of what is beautiful. You only need to look in the mirror with new eyes. With your new eyes you refuse to accept superficial definitions of what beauty is. With your new eyes you are able to look deep inside yourself to find your inner beauty, wisdom, and strength—the essence of who you are. With your new eyes you are able to open yourself to a new thought—that you are already beautiful. There is no need to struggle, no need to contort your body, no need to apply creams or seek cosmetic surgery. All you need to do is simply be beautiful. Simply be.

Loving Yourself

Loving yourself will do more for your appearance than anything else you can do. No cream, no form of exercise, no diet will do what loving yourself will do. The more you love your body, just the way it is, the better you will take care of it, the straighter you will sit and stand, the broader you will smile.

Loving your body is a courageous act. It can cause us to feel as if we are being selfish, self-absorbed, even decadent. Listening to your body's wisdom can feel alien and a little too "new age" for some. Yet these are the things we need to do in order to help our bodies and souls to heal.

1. Begin to focus on taking better care of your physical health. Become more aware of your body and take good care of your physical needs.

2. Just the way a loving parent checks in on a sleeping baby, begin to check in on your body throughout the day. Notice signs of stress, tension, or tiredness; pay attention to whether you are hungry; and ask yourself whether you are feeling sick or healthy.

3. If you notice that you are tense or stressed, find ways to relax your body (stretching, meditation, a nap). If you find that you are hungry, eat a nutritious snack or meal. If you are feeling sick, take some extra vitamins, an herbal remedy or an aspirin, or lie down for a rest.

4. Periodically take an inventory of your body. Notice your posture; are you sitting all slumped over or sitting up nice and straight? Are you holding your muscles or parts of your body tight or are you relaxed? How is your breathing? Full and relaxed or short and labored?

5. Determine that you are going to attend to your body's needs for nourishing food, physical activity, and sleep.

6. Check in periodically with your emotional needs. If you are lonely, make a connection with someone. If you are angry, give yourself permission to express it in constructive ways and to take action to change the situation. If you feel guilty, apologize or make amends to the ones you have hurt or offended.

You cannot expect yourself to love yourself if you don't love your body. Your body is the most precious gift you have. Don't continue to treat it the way your parents or other caretakers did. Don't continue to ignore its needs. Listen to your body. It will tell you what it needs. Show gratitude for all your body provides for you. Honor your body, and it will continue to serve you.

Psychological Truths of the Week

- People who were emotionally abused or neglected tend to be disconnected from their emotions and their bodies. Through body-image and feelings exercises, survivors can reconnect with these important aspects of themselves.

- Children mirror what they see in life, especially what their parents do. Parents who behave in inappropriate ways become unhealthy role models for their children.

MIRROR THERAPY ASSIGNMENT #10: LOOKING AT THE MIRROR WITH NEW EYES

1. Stand in front of a full-length mirror. Close your eyes and breathe deeply. Pretend, just for a moment, that you love yourself just the way you are, especially your body. Inhale and really take in how this would feel, the sense of well-being that comes from total acceptance.

2. Exhale and with it let go of all the shame you've experienced all your life. Let go of all the criticisms, put-downs, and "shoulds" you've heard.

3. Repeat this cycle—inhaling self-acceptance, exhaling shame, criticism, and shoulds.

4. Allow your body to rearrange itself; feel proud, free, strong, and loved with each exhalation and inhalation. Repeat as many times as you need in order to expel the shame and take in the love.

5. Open your eyes and look at yourself. How do you look now?

PART FOUR

Specialized Help

11

If You Were Neglected, Rejected, or Abandoned

Healing the "I Am Unlovable" and "I Am Worthless" Mirrors

Loneliness and the feeling of being unwanted is the most terrible poverty.

—MOTHER TERESA

It is never too late to be what you might have been.

—GEORGE ELIOT

IN THIS CHAPTER I OFFER specific healing strategies for those of you who were neglected, rejected, or abandoned as children. Unfortunately, most victims of childhood neglect and abandonment tend to continue to neglect and abandon themselves as adults. Many survivors don't even know what their needs are, much less how to fulfill them. This is especially true for those who did not receive adequate nurturing from their mothers. If this is your situation, you will need to become your own good mother by providing yourself today with the things you did not receive as a child.

A nurturing mother pays attention to the emotional and physical needs of her children. She makes sure they eat nutritious meals, that they get enough rest and exercise, and most important, that they receive enough hugs and are listened to.

If your need for attention, touch, body acceptance, good nutrition, and exercise were ignored by your mother, or if you did not have a mother in the home, you have likely grown up longing for these things. You may have tried to find mother substitutes in your friends and lovers, and to some degree this may have worked for you. But friends and lovers soon tire of trying to make up for what your mother did not give you. The ones who do not tire of caring for you may take advantage of the situation by being overly controlling or even abusive. The truth is, you are the only one who can give to yourself what you missed out on as a child. Begin by focusing on providing the mothering you need by paying attention to your needs and your body the way a loving mother would care for her child.

Pay Attention to Yourself

If you were hungry or your diapers were wet, your parents probably considered those *real* needs and, hopefully, they fulfilled them. But if what you wanted was attention, that may not have been considered a real need. Today you may treat yourself in the same way. Do you discredit your needs by saying to yourself, "Oh, stop it! All you want is attention," or, "The time for getting those things is over. Grow up!"

If you were neglected or deprived of the things that children need—namely affection, acknowledgment, and protection—you can't expect yourself just to let go of ever getting those needs met. You had to grow up without getting the things you needed, but you were left with some major holes in your development and in your soul. You need to fill up those holes now, today. You need to give to yourself what you missed as a child. In my case, because my mother spent so much time ignoring me and my needs, I needed to start paying attention to my feelings and to what I was needing at any given time. I did this by checking in with myself several times a day, asking myself, "What are you feeling?" and "What do you need?"

Because I was expected to fend for myself at a very early age (four years old), including fixing myself something to eat, I learned very bad habits when it came to food. I had no limits on how much I could eat, and there was always a sense that food was in limited supply. I felt I had better eat as much as I could when it was available in case there wouldn't be any food the next time I was hungry. I needed to become my own good mother by making sure I had lots of healthy food in the house, by cooking myself healthy meals, and by telling myself that I didn't need to gorge myself, because there was plenty of food when I got hungry again.

I also did not have the protection all children need in order to keep themselves safe. My mother slept late in the morning and took naps on her day off. When she wasn't sleeping, she would sit and talk to her friends. This meant I was on my own most of the time. Each day I left my yard and went in search of someone to play with or someone to talk to. This made me vulnerable to sexual abuse (I was molested for the first time when I was four). To make up for this lack of protection as an adult, I needed to start protecting myself better, which in my case meant that I stopped being so reckless with myself (being around people who were not nice to me, driving my car too fast, putting myself in dangerous situations).

Because my mother either ignored me or was critical of me, I needed to pay attention to myself and provide gentle nurturing for myself. I needed to encourage myself in a loving way instead of criticizing my efforts as my mother had. Think of the things you were deprived of as a child and begin to provide them for yourself today.

EXERCISE: PAY ATTENTION TO YOURSELF

Sit in a quiet place. Relax and take a deep breath. Ask yourself, "What sort of attention or nurturing do I need today?" Do you need to acknowledge how hard you have been working on yourself? How much progress you've made in healing your childhood? How about writing yourself an acknowledgment letter? Write to yourself as if you were a loving, nurturing parent, telling her child just how proud she is of what her child has accomplished. Do you feel isolated and alone? You may need to connect with a close friend or a loved one. Are you exhausted from the work week? How about lying down for a few minutes and listening to a CD before starting dinner? How does your body feel? Does your skin need nurturing? How about treating yourself to a facial? Do your feet ache? How about a soothing foot massage? Are your shoulders tense? Fifteen minutes of stretching and breathing exercises would help.

Do this exercise at least once a week in the beginning and work your way up to once a day. You deserve to have attention paid to you.

The Importance of Touch and Human Contact

As we discussed earlier, human touch and support is so vitally important that even infants who are well fed will waste away and even die if their hunger for affection is not satisfied. Feeling unloved and disconnected from those who can provide a reassuring touch or listening ear can permeate our bodies on a cellular level. And yet you may continue to deprive yourself of loving touch and companionship by isolating yourself or pushing away people who would like to get close to you.

Allow Yourself to Feel Your Pain

This is what happened to Susan from chapter 2—the woman who took on very robotic movements due to the severe neglect she experienced from her parents. Susan was so shut down and afraid of being hurt further that she pushed away anyone who tried to get close to her, including me. But gradually, over time, she began to trust me. It took even longer before she began to give to herself the nurturing and care she had missed as a child. At my suggestion, she committed to getting a full body massage once a week by a caring and safe person. This body worker understood how physical neglect can cause a person's body to grow rigid and how much emotional as well as physical resistance Susan would have to being touched. Even though her body and heart were crying out for nurturing, she was afraid of it. More accurately, she was afraid that if she gave in to the pleasure and caring, she would fall apart emotionally, since all the pain of never being touched would finally surface.

Susan's fears were indeed warranted. It was highly likely that once she allowed herself to become physically and emotionally vulnerable, all her pent-up pain would come rushing forth. But with the emotional support of therapy, and the expertise of the body worker, I felt confident that Susan could survive her temporary meltdown and grow from it.

After about three months of weekly massage, Susan's body had become increasingly receptive to touch. Her muscles began to relax and there was a softer look about her, particularly on her face, which now showed just the slightest bit of expression. One day she came in to therapy looking extremely soft. Her face no longer had its typical rigid expression. I asked her what had happened. She told me that during her last massage session she had begun to cry. At first it was just tears seeping from her eyes. But soon she was wailing like a child. She was on her back at the time—the massage therapist had been working on her stomach. She said she felt the sobs coming from deep within her stomach and she needed to roll on her side in order to breathe. The massage therapist covered her up with a blanket and started gently caressing her forehead and head. Susan lay sobbing in the fetal position for what seemed like a long, long time, feeling as if she would never stop. But after what the massage therapist said was about fifteen minutes, she finally began to stop sobbing. The therapist then began massaging Susan's feet, which helped Susan begin to feel more grounded. By the time she got up from the massage table, she felt weak but very relaxed and proud of herself for allowing herself to feel her pain on such a deep level.

Susan needed to feel this pain, and if you suffered in any of the ways that Susan did as a child, you need to allow yourself to feel your pain as well. Weekly massages can help provide the nurturing you and your body so desperately need, but they can also help you lower your defenses so you can allow good things in and your pain to come out.

Abandonment Wounds

Neglect, rejection, and abandonment (physical and emotional) all create severe emotional wounds in a child. These abandonment wounds can create a lifetime of feeling that there is something inherently wrong with oneself.

If you suffer from these deep abandonment wounds, you need to make sure you don't continue to abandon *yourself* the way you were abandoned as a child. You abandon yourself when you put yourself in dangerous or hurtful situations, when you don't provide proper nutrition and adequate rest for yourself, and when you don't allow yourself to speak up in your own behalf. Learning that the adult part of you can actually give to the child part of you what you missed as a child can be an especially powerful way of breaking this abandonment pattern.

It can be very painful to be told that you are not likely to receive from your parents the love, attention, and validation you missed out on as a child, no matter how hard you try to please your parents today. Many who were neglected or abandoned spend their entire lives looking to their parents or others to give to them today what they didn't get as a child. Some stay tied to their neglectful parents and continue to suffer from the pain of rejection, abandonment, or disappointment. Others have the expectation that others should take away their pain. This causes them constant disappointment as well as further experiences of rejection and abandonment. I want to save you from both of these tragedies. The best way to do this is to stress to you that you absolutely must stop expecting others to take care of you.

Even though no one else can give you what you missed as a child, this doesn't mean you are doomed to never receive it. There is one person who can give you what you missed out on—what you so desperately need and desire. That person is you.

The adult part of you—that part who had to grow up even though you didn't get what you needed to do so—can begin to take care of the needy child in you. The adult part takes care of business, gets up to go to work every day, pays the bills, and puts a roof over your head. This adult part of you can begin to take care of the child part of you—the part who feels helpless, afraid, deprived, and unloved.

Inner-Child Work

The concept of inner-child work was developed many years ago, and numerous therapists, particularly those who work in the recovery field, have been recommending inner-child techniques for so long that they have become somewhat of a cliché. But cliché or not, inner-child work can be the most important work that people who were neglected or abandoned can do to raise their self-esteem.

The concept of the inner child is the idea that we all hold within ourselves the memory or the essence of the child we once were. It is as if one part of us grew up and became an adult, but another part of us remained a child. This is particularly true of people who were neglected or abused as children, because neglect and abuse can cause us to become fixated or stuck at a certain age—unable or unwilling to grow up. Our inner child is also symbolic of our feeling selves. Accessing this feeling self can help you to determine what you need at any given time.

EXERCISE: DISCOVER YOUR INNER CHILD

The following are suggestions as to how you can discover and nurture your inner child:

1. Go through old picture albums, paying particular attention to photos of yourself as a child. Look closely at them and find one or two that you are attracted to, either because you have feelings of fondness or tenderness toward the child in the photo or because there is something particularly compelling about the child you see.

2. Get this picture framed and put it up in your bedroom or another room where you will see it often. Or place a photo of yourself as a child on your bedroom or bathroom mirror as a subtle reminder that you have a deprived child inside you who needs love. Actually speaking to that picture of yourself every morning, saying things like "I am with you," "I will take care of you," and "I love you" can be extremely healing.

3. Begin to imagine that your inner child is with you at all times and that this child has needs you must attend to. For example, picturing your inner child next to you in your car can cause you to drive safer or take time out to stop for lunch.

4. Begin carrying on a dialogue with your inner child. For example, you might ask, "How are you feeling today?" or "What do you want to do today?" Most people do this silently, inside their heads, but others actually speak out loud to their inner children and have them answer out loud.

EXERCISE: A WRITTEN DIALOGUE WITH YOUR INNER CHILD

An effective way of beginning a dialogue with your inner child is to do the following writing exercise:

1. Draw a vertical line down the center of a piece of paper or on a page in your journal.

2. With your dominant hand (if you are right-handed, this will be your right hand) ask your child a simple question like "How are you feeling today?" or simply write, "Hello." Write this on the left side of the vertical line.

3. Switch your pen or pencil to your less dominant hand and see if an answer comes to you. Don't overthink it. See if something just flows out. The answer generally feels as if it is from another part of you. In this case, we are focusing on your inner child, so the answer may very well sound childlike. Write this answer on the right side of the vertical line.

4. If your inner child is trusting and accessible, he or she might say something like "I'm sad" or "Hello" in response. But often there is no response at all. This may be an indication that your inner child is angry with you or does not trust you enough to respond. Because you haven't connected to your inner child before, she or he naturally may feel suspicious of you. After all, where have you been? Why haven't you cared about her before? For this reason, you may need to ask several times, on different occasions, before your inner child trusts that you really care. Some people have actually gotten a response such as, "What do you care?" or "I'm not going to talk to you."

Connecting with Your Inner Child

Many people have a difficult time finding their inner child. If this is true for you, you may need to gain your inner child's trust before she reveals herself to you, because many adults who were neglected or abused began treating their inner child the same way their parents treated them. As my client Dana explained to me, "My mother ignored me and my needs. She simply pretended I wasn't there. Now I find that I do the same thing to my inner child. I just ignore her, hoping she'll just leave me alone." If you've been ignoring your inner child and her needs for a long time, she isn't likely to reveal herself to you very readily. After all, why should she? As another client, Toni, explained it, "My inner child didn't want anything to do with me. She didn't trust me as far as she could throw me. Every time I tried talking to her I just heard a deadly silence."

You may have to earn your inner child's trust. You do this by being consistent and patient and by keeping your promises. Don't ask your inner child what she wants or needs unless you plan on providing it for her. And never, ever tell your inner child you are going to do something and then not do it. Whatever blossoming trust she may have had in you will go right out the window. The following suggestions will help you connect with even the most reticent inner child.

1. If you continue to get no response when you attempt a written dialogue, you may wish to write a letter to your inner child. The purpose is for you to make contact, to express any regrets you have about the way your child was treated and about the way you continue to treat him or her. If you are sincere and genuinely sorry, your child is more likely to gain some trust in you.

2. You may then attempt to have your inner child write a letter back to you. You can do this using your less dominant hand if you wish, but it is not necessary.

All of this may sound foolish to you, but believe me, these techniques really work. Not only do they help you to connect with the disowned parts of yourself (your feelings, your childhood memories), but they also help you to focus on taking better care of your needs. In essence, they help you to provide for yourself today what you didn't receive from your parents when you were growing up.

Self-Indulgence

Adult children who were deprived in childhood not only continue to deprive themselves the way their parents did, but they also often go to the other extreme and become overly self-indulgent. In fact, the flip side of deprivation is indulgence. This is why so many neglected and emotionally abused children grow up to become adults who are overindulgent. As a way of balancing their hardships, and in a desperate need to comfort themselves, they develop a way of being far too easy on themselves. When life becomes difficult, they look to food, alcohol, drugs, relationships, shopping, or a multitude of other addictions for solace and comfort. Based on in-depth interviews with the families of obese children, Hilde Bruch, a psychiatrist at Baylor College of Medicine, and her colleague, Grace Touraine, found that the roots of the drive to go to excess were parenting styles that were permissive and/or depriving. Medical literature has since corroborated Bruch's and Touraine's findings, showing that various problems are more likely to arise when parents are permissive or depriving. The literature on eating disorders, substance abuse, affective disorders, and health promotion is particularly consistent with this idea.

My Experience with Deprivation and Indulgence

My mother was a single parent who worked hard to support us. She stood on her feet for eight hours a day, selling cosmetics to wealthy women in an upscale department store. Every day she got up several hours early to give herself plenty of time to apply full makeup and dress immaculately so she would look good for her job. She was so focused on looking good in order to keep her job that she paid little attention to what I wore or even to making certain that I took care of basic hygiene, such as brushing my teeth. The result was that I often went around with dirty teeth, dirty hair, and unclean clothes.

Because my mother worked so hard and was so stressed out over keeping her job and putting food on the table, she indulged herself in the evenings and on her days off. One of the first things she did when she got home was to open her first of many cans of beer and sit down to watch TV. On her days off she allowed herself to sleep in—often until noon. When she finally got up, she drank coffee and smoked cigarettes for several hours until she segued into drinking beer and smoking cigarettes late in the afternoon. She read or watched TV for the rest of the evening—sometimes drinking as much as two six-packs of beer.

As a child I felt horribly deprived of a mother. I longed for one who would get up in the morning and do what I saw other mothers doing—making breakfast, cleaning the house, doing their kids' laundry. I wanted to be able to bring my friends over for dinner, have my mother drive us to a movie, or go bowling, as my friends' mothers would do with them. Instead, I got up in the morning and went outside to find a neighborhood kid to play with or an adult to talk to. On school days I got myself dressed and went off to school without breakfast. I often looked like a little ragamuffin.

You'd think that I would be a thin, maybe even sickly child, but fortunately I had good genes and maintained fairly good health, with the exception of suffering from chronic bronchitis because of my mother's smoking. I also had severe constipation because I ate so little in the way of vegetables and fruit, and I had multiple cavities because of my poor dental hygiene. Instead of being thin, by the time I reached six or seven I began to look rather pudgy. I had already begun to indulge myself with food in order to make up for the emotional deprivation I experienced. Ravenous from missing breakfast, I would scarf down every bite of my cafeteria lunch. After school I made myself fried egg sandwiches (we never had lunch meats or cheese on hand). At dinner I stuffed myself with whatever my mother had managed to put together. And late in the evening I would sneak into the refrigerator to see what I could find.

The beginnings of my tendency to indulge myself also came from my mother's tendency to go to extremes with deprivation and indulgence. We would "scrape by," as she would say, all week, eating beans and macaroni, but when she got her paycheck she would always buy us a steak or a chicken and a treat. This was usually a half gallon of ice milk—a cheaper version of ice cream. She'd buy the ice milk on a Friday, for example, and by Saturday night, or at the latest by Sunday afternoon, it would be gone. She would probably have one bowl of it and I would have the rest.

From my mother I learned many things. I learned to work hard. In fact, I learned that you can do most anything if you just forge ahead and put your mind to it. She was able to raise a child all on her own in spite of the fact that she didn't have any skills except being a good salesperson. I learned that if you just stayed focused on the task at hand and ignored your body, your feelings, and your needs, you could get by with little rest, little pleasure, and little nurturing. And this is what I became accustomed to doing for most of my life. I worked hard and accomplished wonderful things, but seldom took the time to pay attention to my body or my emotional needs. I deprived myself of sleep and seldom played or gave myself much pleasure. I ended up doing the same as my mother—dividing my life into two extremes: deprivation and indulgence. I worked myself into exhaustion and then "came down" from my work frenzy by overeating and then "sleeping it off." Just as my mother dealt with stress by drinking her six-packs, I dealt with mine by overeating when I got home. And surprise, surprise, at the end of a long week at work I "rewarded" myself with ice cream.

Journaling Exercise: Too Harsh or Too Easy

1. Write about the ways that you are too easy on yourself (you don't push yourself to exercise, you allow yourself to eat ice cream even though you want to lose weight, or you continue to allow yourself to procrastinate).

2. Write about the ways that you are too harsh with yourself (pushing yourself to complete a task and ignoring your need for proper nutrition and rest, depriving yourself of a treat now and then because you are so obsessed with staying thin).

Stop Attacking Yourself

Few childhood experiences have as destructive an impact on your sense of self as abandonment. It creates a basic feeling of worthlessness or wrongness that amplifies even mild hurts into a feeling of devastation. If you were abandoned as a child, almost any painful event can cause you to experience a sinking feeling of worthlessness. For example, if someone becomes critical or angry with you, if you feel ignored or discounted, or if you make a mistake, it can confirm your basic belief that you are worthless. Your reaction may be either to get angry at yourself and chastise yourself severely or to become numb. You may live in constant fear that others will discover how worthless you really are. When someone criticizes or rejects you, it may feel as if they have seen the real you. No matter how small the current difficulty, it is a painful reminder of the times when you were rejected or abandoned as a child and came to believe that you were to blame for it.

Even though you may try to tell yourself that it is just a small thing, your reasonable voice gets drowned out by your overwhelming feelings of worthlessness and being wrong. You may try to defend against or block the feelings of worthlessness by attacking yourself, believing that if you beat yourself up enough you will finally correct your flaws—that the things you hate in yourself can be fixed—and that when you have beaten yourself into shape the bad feeling will go away.

This kind of self-flagellation can actually work temporarily. You are so focused on correcting your flaws that the deep feeling of not being okay gets masked for awhile. But over time you are further destroying your self-esteem and self-worth.

The only way to stop these self-attacks is to realize that every time you beat yourself up you are not only damaging your self-worth but you are also running away from reality. You are creating a fantasy in which you believe you can finally carve yourself into your personal ideal. But you cannot cut and hack yourself into shape. In fact, you are doing more harm than good. Self-attack actually reduces your capacity to change. It is only when you feel good about yourself that you feel motivated to make real changes.

Redirect Your Anger

Many people who were abandoned in childhood turn their rage over being abandoned against themselves in the form of self-blame, self-punishment, or self-loathing. If you are one of them, it is vitally important that you work on redirecting your anger toward those who abandoned you.

When Nancy was six years old, her parents divorced. Nancy's father moved across the country, and her mother left her in the care of her grandmother while she looked for work. She couldn't find a job in their small town but was able to get one in a nearby city. Unfortunately, because she felt that the city was no place to raise a child, she left Nancy with her grandmother full time and visited her every weekend. Nancy grew up feeling abandoned by both her parents but particularly by her mother, whose visits became more and more infrequent.

As is typical of children, Nancy blamed herself for her mother's abandonment. She felt that if she had been a better daughter, her mother would have wanted to take her back to the city. Each time Nancy's mother left her, Nancy searched her brain, trying to discover what she had done wrong. As an adult, Nancy continued to blame herself for her mother's abandonment. She was convinced that there was something inherently wrong with her and that no man would want her because of it. When I met Nancy she was a lonely woman with few friends who tended to be terribly self-critical.

It didn't take long to realize that Nancy needed to get angry at her mother for abandoning her and for not loving her enough to make time for her. She needed to recognize that her mother left her because she was selfish or not a good mother, not because Nancy was not a good daughter.

With some encouragement from me, Nancy was finally able to face the truth about her mother. In one of our role-playing sessions she was able to say to her mother, "I'm not worthless. You are the one who was worthless. You were a worthless mother." In this session Nancy made a huge step toward her recovery.

Do you remember Tammy from chapter 2—the cutter? A significant part of her recovery was her acknowledgment of how angry she was at her abandoning father. Instead of internalizing the rejection and assuming that there must have been something wrong with her to cause her father to reject her, she was finally able to allow herself to get angry with him and to begin to recognize that it was he who had the problem.

Earlier I shared with you that Tammy hated to see her reflection in the mirror. As a matter of fact, she hated her image so much that several times in the past she had actually smashed mirrors—sometimes with her bare fists, other times by throwing an object at it. "I'd become enraged when I saw myself. I felt so unacceptable and unlovable. And I felt so guilty for the way I was treating myself [the cutting]. But I didn't know how to stop myself." By turning her righteous anger on her father instead of on herself, Tammy began to recognize that the problem was not with her but with her father. "There is something wrong with him. After all, what kind of a father rejects his own daughter?"

Stop Protecting Your Parents

You met Greg in chapter 2. He was the boy whose mother suffered from severe headaches around him and who expected Greg to take care of her instead of the other way around. Greg needed to get angry at his mother for her neglect, but like many children of inadequate parents, he had a difficult time acknowledging his anger. Because their parents often behave like helpless or irresponsible children, adult children tend to feel protective of them and to jump to their parents' defense if anyone criticizes them. "But they didn't mean any harm" and "They did the best they could" are often the typical responses. This was the case with Greg. When I pointed out to him that his mother had abdicated her responsibilities to him, he became very angry—at me. "My mother couldn't help it that she had those bad headaches. She was completely debilitated by them." When I pointed out that he had told me that his mother never seemed to have those headaches when his father came home and that, in fact, she seemed to be miraculously cured just before his arrival, Greg countered with, "Well, maybe I was confused about that. Maybe it didn't really happen that way."

It took a while before Greg was able to understand that he had been forced to grow up too soon and that he had been robbed of a childhood. He needed to stop exhausting himself by taking care of his mother and start focusing on his own needs for a change. Once he did this, Greg noticed that he had a lot more energy. "I used to feel weighted down with responsibility. Now I feel a new freedom. For the first time in my life, I'm getting in touch with what I want and need at any particular time. And I feel so much better about myself. My self-esteem used to always be tied in with how much my mother loved me and how much I was able to accomplish. Now my self-esteem comes from taking care of my own needs."

Being Reminded of Your Value and Lovability

It is generally not a good idea to look outside of yourself in order to feel good about who you are. But people who experienced abandonment (and/or extreme criticism) as children tend to need external validation more than others. This need for external validation is understandable, because if you were abandoned by your parents you were *invalidated*. When the ones who are most important to you in your life don't seem to love, value, or accept you, you will obviously feel unwanted and unworthy. As a result, you will feel desperate to be reassured that you are in fact lovable, valued, and appreciated. Although no one can bestow self-esteem on you, the validation of friends and lovers can help you feel better about yourself so that you can bestow esteem on yourself. In other words, using external validation can become a tool for helping you raise your self-esteem.

JOURNALING EXERCISE: FROM EXTERNAL VALIDATION TO SELF-ESTEEM

The next time you make a mistake or are overwhelmed with feelings of worthlessness for any reason, do the following journaling exercise:

1. Remember a time when you were acknowledged by friends, family, or others in your community for something you did well.
2. How did getting this feedback feel?
3. What do your friends seem to value most in you?

4. Think of a close friend. What do you imagine he or she might say if asked the question, "What do you value most about me?"

5. What do you value most about yourself?

6. Does your friend's appraisal of you match your own? How?

7. Is there anything about yourself that you value but your friends don't seem to recognize?

8. What additional qualities about yourself would you like others to recognize?

12

If You Were Overprotected or Emotionally Smothered

Healing the "I Am Nothing without My Parent" Mirror

> *You love me so much, you want to put me in your pocket.*
> *And I should die there smothered.*
>
> —D. H. LAWRENCE

OVERLY PROTECTIVE OR SMOTHERING parents tend to deprive their children of energy and an awareness of their own separate identity, leaving them no strength to grow and develop their unique personalities. Parents who refuse to let their children separate from them are actually restricting and limiting their child's potential to make something of themselves in the world. When a parent's desire to protect goes too far, it can block the development of the child and severely limit his or her choices in the world.

One of the primary problems adults who were overprotected or emotionally smothered tend to experience is difficulty separating and individuating from their parents. The term *separation* refers to the ability to have a clear psychic representation (an internal image and understanding) of the self as different from everyone else, especially the mother. Many who were overly protected or emotionally smothered, especially by their mothers, tend to continue to regard themselves as extensions of their mothers.

Separation is especially difficult when parents are not able to let their children be separate and when they continue to consider them as extensions of themselves, discouraging any attempts on the children's part to become separate. This is especially true of parents with narcissistic tendencies or a narcissistic personality disorder.

The term *individuation* refers to identity formation. It is not sufficient just to separate; you also need to have a clear image and understanding of who you are. In order to do this, those who were overly protected or emotionally smothered often need to freely and consciously choose who they want to be instead of taking on certain characteristics, beliefs, values, and attitudes to please their parents.

Narcissistic, overly protective, and emotionally smothering parents tend to insist on obedience, to foster dependency, and to quickly stomp on any signs of resistance and rebellion. But resisting and rebelling are often exactly what adult children of these kinds of parents need to do if they are to develop a separate sense of self.

This was the case with Lupe, whom you met in chapter 2. She not only lacked the strength to stand up to her father and fight for what she wanted, but also she doubted her own ability to make the right decisions for herself. When I encouraged her to begin thinking for herself, she told me, "You know, my father is usually right about things. If I did what I wanted to do, I'd probably mess up my life."

It took many months of therapy before Lupe was able to admit that she resented her father's smothering, controlling ways. It took even more therapy before she could express her anger toward him during role-playing sessions with me. Even then she felt a bit guilty about doing so. "I feel like a rebellious teenager—but I guess that's appropriate, since I didn't get to rebel as a kid."

Joshua: The Case of the "Momma's Boy"

Joshua is an eighteen-year-old who came to see me because of a recent breakup with his girlfriend. He had been suffering from depression ever since the relationship ended. "I just can't seem to bounce back like I should. I'm still angry with my ex and I have no interest in getting involved with any other girls. I've even started wondering whether I am capable of really loving another person."

Over the course of several weeks, Joshua and I delved deeper into his feelings. It turned out that he didn't like himself very much. "I'm really disappointed in myself. There are so many things I want to do but I'm too afraid to try them." We also explored his family background. Joshua was raised by a workaholic father who seldom spent time with him and an overly controlling, smothering mother.

"My mother worries a lot," Joshua explained. "She wants to know what I am doing at all times—who my friends are and what we are doing. She monitors what I watch on TV and how I use the computer—not just the normal monitoring but in an extreme way. Ever since I was a little kid she always had chores for me to do, and if I resisted in any way she put a real guilt-trip on me about how overworked she was. I was the youngest of five kids. By the time she'd had me she was tired—I understood that. So I tried to help her out. But I had to do things just a certain way to please her. My brothers think I'm a momma's boy because I stayed home with my mother so much. But it isn't because I am so close to her—it is because I didn't feel I had a right to my own life. And it was because my mother trained me to comply with her wishes. In reality I resent her for being so controlling. And I hate myself for not standing up to her more."

What Joshua discovered was that there was a connection between his strong dislike and disappointment in himself, his inability to really open up and care for another human being, and the way his mother controlled and monitored him. Because he couldn't stand up to his mother and refuse her demands, Joshua didn't respect himself. Because he didn't respect himself but viewed himself as a weakling, he didn't like himself—much less love himself. And because he wasn't able to love himself, he couldn't love anyone else. Making this connection was very profound for Joshua.

Now, as Joshua explained it, "I'm trying to break free." He questions things instead of just going along with his mother's demands, and he doesn't give in to his mother's codependent behavior (like having to listen to her problems). He lets her know that while he understands her worries, she needs to begin to trust him, since he has proven to her time and again that he is trustworthy. He is finding that the more he stands up for himself with his mother, the more he is able to stand up to others. "I'm not the little weakling anymore," he boasted one day. "I even stood up to my bully of a brother!"

Joshua likes himself more and more as time goes by, and this is affecting his ability to care about others. "I'm not so angry with my ex-girlfriend anymore. In fact, I can see where she was coming from. I wasn't ready for a relationship and she sensed it. I think I'll be a lot more able to love in my next relationship because I like myself so much better."

Healing from Emotional Incest

In order to heal from the damage of emotional incest, you first need to admit that you are a victim of it. This can be especially difficult, because many adults who had an emotionally incestuous parent are in denial or are unaware of the negative consequences of such a relationship. Instead, all they focus on are the things they gained from it, namely, extra privileges, a close relationship with a parent, praise and affection, shared confidences, and/or patient tutoring. After all, every child wishes he or she had this kind of special relationship with an opposite-sex parent.

QUESTIONNAIRE: SIGNS OF EMOTIONAL INCEST

Read each of the following statements and put a checkmark next to the ones that apply to you. You may find it helpful to put the initials of the parent or caregiver next to each statement.

1. I was a source of emotional support for one of my parents.

2. I was "best friends" with a parent.

3. When one of my parents left the home (either due to divorce, death, or long absences), I was told that I needed to take his or her place (for boys, to be "the man of the house," or for girls, to "keep daddy company").

4. I was given special privileges or gifts by one of my parents.

5. A parent told me that I was better company than his or her spouse.

6. A parent told me that I understood him or her more than his or her spouse.

7. A parent talked to me about his or her problems.

8. A parent told me secrets and made me promise not to tell my other parent.

9. One of my parents told me in confidence that I was his or her favorite child.

10. One of my parents told me he or she wished my other parent was more like me.

11. One of my parents felt lonely a lot and needed me to keep him or her company.

12. I felt I had to protect or take care of one of my parents.

13. A parent relied on me more than on any of my siblings.

14. I felt responsible for my parent's happiness.

15. I sometimes feel guilty when I spend time away from one of my parents.

16. I got the impression that a parent did not want me to move away from home or to marry.

17. No one who ever dated me was good enough for one of my parents.

18. One of my parents seemed to be overly concerned about my developing sexuality.

19. I sometimes got the feeling that one of my parents had romantic or sexual feelings toward me.

20. One of my parents made inappropriate sexual remarks or violated my privacy.

If you answered yes to any of these questions, you probably had a codependent relationship with a needy parent. But if you consistently answered yes to these questions, you also suffered from emotional incest. This is especially true if you answered yes to questions 2 through 10 and 18 through 20.

Confronting the fact that you were a victim of emotional incest and that there are indeed negative consequences to such extreme devotion can be unsettling. But by doing so you will gain insight into some of your most puzzling and troublesome emotional problems.

What are the negative consequences, particularly as related to your self-esteem? According to Dr. Patricia Love, the author of *The Emotional Incest Syndrome*, and other experts on emotional incest, the major effects emotional incest has on self-esteem and self-image include:

1. Self-image problems: dramatic shifts in self-esteem. You can be full of confidence one moment and overcome with inadequacy the next.

2. Excessive guilt over any and all of the following: taking a parent away from a partner, being treated better than your siblings, failing to live up to your parent's expectations, wanting to break away from an overbearing or smothering parent (or managing to do so). All this guilt can eat away at your self-esteem.

3. Chronic anxiety and fear of rejection owing to any of the following: Your role as the chosen child or surrogate partner was always uncertain. Your bond with your parent was a secret, denied by your parent and the rest of the family as well. And you may have sensed that your role as surrogate spouse may have only been temporary. If your parents resolved their problems, you may have been forced to return to your role as a child. Or one of your siblings may have replaced you, causing you to wonder, "What's wrong with me? Aren't I still special?" If your parent was married, you always had to step aside to make room for the legitimate marriage partner. For fear of becoming sexually involved, a parent of the opposite sex may withdraw when the child shows signs of sexual maturity, leaving the child to feel rejected. If you were able to develop some sense of independence from your parent, he or she may have been threatened by your emerging sense of self and may have become critical or rejecting.

4. Your fundamental needs for nurturing and independence were ignored in favor of your parent's need for intimacy and

companionship. This may have left you feeling deprived and needy and yet feeling guilty for feeling these things. It also can cause you to minimize your own needs in favor of taking care of the needs of others.

5. Your parent's excessive interest in you may have created a need to be taken care of or paid attention to. When there is no one around to do things with you or for you, you may feel deprived.

6. Your parent's intense, inappropriate attention may have left you feeling confined and unable to develop your own self, and at your own pace.

Action Steps for Healing

Whether you were overprotected, emotionally smothered, or emotionally incested, there are specific things you need to do in order to emotionally separate from your parent and raise your self-esteem:

1. Determine your comfort level in terms of how often you wish to see your parent. You and you alone need to determine the frequency and conditions. For example, some people are more comfortable visiting their parents at the parents' home, because they can leave when they become uncomfortable and they don't like their parent invading their personal space. While you may feel obligated to see your parents on holidays and other special occasions, you need to do so only if you can maintain your personal boundaries.

2. Set limits around an invasive parent. Personal boundaries include how close you allow your parent to get to you physically, what you wish to share with him or her about your personal life, and what you are willing to listen to about your parent's personal life. Spend some time determining what your comfort level is around these issues and then reinforce these boundaries when in your parent's presence.

3. Figure out your role in the continuing boundary violation. For example, do you have a misplaced sense of guilt? Do you feel overly responsible for your parent? These are common reactions when a parent has made it abundantly clear that he or she made huge sacrifices for a child. And a child who was trained to take care of a parent's emotional needs will have a hard time letting go of this role. But it is very important that you stop buying into this guilt. You are an adult who deserves her own life separate from your parent. You do not owe your parent so much that you need to sacrifice your own life for that person.

4. Don't continue to ask for help from a smothering parent. If your parent already feels he or she has a right to tell you what you should do, do not encourage this behavior by asking for advice or assistance. You need to let your smothering parent know that you are a capable and competent adult. You do not convey this message if you periodically look to your parent to rescue you emotionally or financially.

5. Speak up the moment your boundaries are violated. State your position calmly and clearly. For example, "Dad, I want you to call me before you come over," or "Mom, please don't call me at work. Call me at home instead."

13

If You Were Overly Controlled or Tyrannized

Healing the "I Am Powerless" Mirror

You were once wild here. Don't let them tame you!

—Isadora Duncan

Freedom is what you do with what's been done to you.

—Jean-Paul Sartre

In this chapter I will help those of you who were overly controlled or tyrannized to break free from your parent's domination, discover your own power, and take it back. This begins with telling your story. Although sharing what happened to you in childhood is important for anyone who was emotionally abused or neglected, it is particularly meaningful for those who were overly controlled or tyrannized. By telling your story you will make it more real and thus rid yourself of any lingering denial, air long-suppressed feelings, and come to better understand your behavior and beliefs. Since you probably had a childhood of not being able to speak up or defend yourself, doing so now can also validate your experience and help to empower you. And by telling your story you are giving yourself what you did not receive in childhood—the chance to talk without interruption, the experience of being seen and heard as you really are, and the opportunity to be validated. Here are some suggestions for finding safe ways and safe environments in which to tell your story:

1. Find a therapist or lay counselor you trust and tell her or him about your abusive childhood.

2. Ask your partner or a trusted friend if he or she would be willing to hear your story. Set a time when both of you have at least an hour to devote to this, uninterrupted. Ask your friend just to listen and not make any comments until you are finished. Tell this person that you don't need to have your problems solved for you, just a loving and sympathetic ear.

3. Write down your story or record it on audio- or videotape. Don't censor yourself, just tell the truth and how it made you feel. Later you can read or listen to your story for even more healing. Make sure you read or listen without judgment and with compassion for yourself.

Make Sure You Aren't Still Being Controlled

In order to raise your self-esteem and take back your power, you also need to make sure you are not still being controlled by your parents, or anyone else for that matter. While it is completely understandable that you would be susceptible to allowing others to control you, you will never feel good about yourself as long as you allow it. You will lose respect for yourself each time you allow someone to control you, and if you continue, you will eventually feel nothing but self-loathing.

In order to take back their power from controlling parents, adult children must emotionally separate from those parents. Sometimes this means confronting them; other times it means setting healthier boundaries. Setting appropriate boundaries today can provide empowerment by balancing childhood boundary violations. It may also involve reducing contact with parents. Controlling parents chose when they had access to their children. Altering that access can empower you by showing you that you now have control over when you see your parents and what kind of interaction you are willing to have.

Another act of empowerment is being able to see parents for who they are today. Often adult children of controlling parents continue to see them as larger-than-life characters who still have the power to control them. By beginning to see your parents more accurately, you can begin to take away some of the power they have over you. This may include standing next to a parent and noticing how much smaller he or she is than the picture you have in your mind. It also helps to have someone take a picture of you with your parent so you are confronted with the fact that you are now physically as big as or bigger than your parent.

Equalization also comes from letting go of needs and expectations concerning your parents, including the false hope that they will finally accept you as you are or give you what they didn't provide for you as a child. As you give up your emotional attachment to what your parent should have been, you may find you are left with a relationship with a mere man or woman instead of the monster or the icon you had perceived your parent to be.

How to Take Back Your Power

The best way to take back your power is to confront your parents about their abusive behavior. Although you still may be afraid to do this directly, you can do so by imagining that you are confronting your parents and telling them how you really feel.

Lorraine is the woman from chapter 4 who was humiliated for not getting the scuffs off the floor. Although she was still afraid of her mother, it helped when she finally gave herself permission to express her anger toward her mother during our sessions. "Even though she isn't going to hear what I am saying, I guess I have the fear that she'll somehow know. I know it's stupid. And I feel so disloyal to her when I get angry. After all, I know she was doing the best she could." Lorraine was eventually able to put aside these unnecessary concerns and express to me how she really felt about her mother's treatment of her. "I hated her for treating me so badly," she told me with real anger in her voice. "She expected too much of me. I was just a little kid. No one should be talked to or treated like that."

This was the beginning of Lorraine's ability to separate from her mother. The next step was to confront her mother directly, which was extremely frightening. "I don't know what I think she's going to do to me. After all, she's a little old lady now. She can't beat me anymore. She probably can't even yell at me. Why am I so afraid?"

Create a Protector

To help Lorraine face her mother, I encouraged her to create what I call a "protector"—an imaginary person who will stand beside you or behind you when you do difficult things. Creating a protector can give you the necessary courage to stand up to your tyrannical parent. The following exercise will explain this concept further.

EXERCISE: CREATING A PROTECTOR

1. Imagine that there is someone standing behind you, someone who is there to protect you and stand up for you against anyone who criticizes you, attacks you, or puts you down.

2. Remember an incident in your childhood when one of your parents (or other caregiver) criticized or shamed you.

3. Imagine what your protector would say to this person. Imagine the words he or she would use to push the negative, critical statements away.

4. If you feel like it, say those words out loud.

Creating a protector helped Lorraine to confront her mother: "I know it seems funny, but it gave me the strength to face her, knowing that I wasn't alone."

When I asked my client Stephen to imagine that a protector was standing behind him, someone who would stand up to his emotionally abusive mother, he broke down and sobbed. Normally Stephen had difficulty crying, much less sobbing. I felt deeply moved by his sobs and sorrow—so much so that I went over to the couch where he sat and put my hand gently on his shoulder. Once the sobs subsided,

Stephen said, "I never had anyone like that—I never had anyone who stood up for me or protected me."

Quiet Your Inner Critic

People who were overly controlled or tyrannized tend to develop a particularly powerful inner critic. Because you were so controlled and tyrannized, you had no choice but to internalize your parents' critical voices. Therefore, in order to heal and raise your self-esteem you will need to find powerful ways to quiet your critical inner messages.

Start by looking at your self-criticisms. Are you criticizing yourself today the way you were criticized as a child? The themes of your inner critic—those "voice-overs" installed by your parents—are often loudest when you are acting or feeling counter to your parents' values or rules. By naming these voices—"Oh, that's my mother's controlling voice again,"—you can actually take away some of their power. Your goal is not to banish the self-critical messages from your head but to get to know your inner critic and how it works, and to set limits on its influence.

Once you have set healthier limits on both your inner parental voices and your actual parents, you will find that you have a greater capacity to hear another voice inside yourself—your nurturing voice. Following are some suggestions for limiting your inner critic:

- Whenever you hear a critical message, say, "No! I don't want to hear it!" or "No, I don't believe you."

- Counter any critical messages with self-praise. For example: "No, I'm not lazy. Look at all the work I've done today. I'm a hard worker."

- Don't allow your parent's critical assessment or unreasonable expectations to rule you. If you tend to drive yourself compulsively in reaction to parents who called you lazy or good for nothing, slow down. Ask yourself if you are working so hard because you want to or to please your parents. If you are underperforming as a way to rebel against your parents' pressure, you may want to push yourself a little more to find some internal motivation. Often those who are rebelling against parents' unreasonable expectations tend to be too easy on themselves. By pushing yourself just a little, you may discover a real desire and sense of accomplishment in creating or completing tasks.

Acknowledge and Feel Your Pain

The judge or inner critic specializes in attacking us for feeling our pain with messages like "What good is it to feel pain? It won't change anything!" "You are such a crybaby," and "Watch out, you might lose it and then you'll really be in a mess!" But unless you are willing to acknowledge and feel your pain at being emotionally abused, you will find it difficult to experience compassion for yourself or others.

Remember, self-compassion is a direct antidote to the judge's poison. The soothing warmth of a nurturing inner voice neutralizes that poison. Tenderness dissolves the harshness and rejection. Call up your nurturing inner voice and talk to yourself with compassion and understanding whenever you are being self-critical or powerless.

Tell Your Story to a Compassionate Witness

Voicing your story to a someone who cares will help you receive some of the empathetic mirroring you may have missed out on in childhood. It also provides a way for you to give yourself other things you missed out on in childhood, namely the experience of being seen and heard as you really are (without your parent's distorted perceptions blocking your view) and the opportunity to be validated.

How Being in Touch with Your Essence Can Help You Quiet Your Inner Critic

According to Byron Brown, the author of *Soul without Shame*, your inner critic generally recognizes the importance of essential human qualities, but it does not believe that you have them innately. Instead, it tells you that you must acquire them from the outside through accomplishments and good behavior: "If you are a kind, giving person then perhaps you have some value."

In order to confront your inner critic's dominance in guiding and controlling your experience, you must first recognize that your essence is not the result of your accomplishments or effect on others. It is and has always been a part of you. You also need to see how your inner critic continually undermines such an awareness. Then you must call upon specific qualities of your essence or true nature to challenge the way your inner critic operates. As you recognize and develop your contact with these aspects of your humanness, you will discover an alternative guidance and support system that is grounded in a more fundamental sense of reality.

Continue to Develop Self-Acceptance and Self-Love

In order to cancel out all the negative esteem-robbing comments made to you by your controlling or tyrannical parents, you will need to continue to work on self-acceptance and self-love. You met my client Marilyn earlier in the book. (She was unable to look into the mirror other than a quick glance when she combed her hair or put on makeup.) When I suggested she try to look in the mirror for a slightly longer period of time, she balked. "I can't. I just can't. I don't want to see myself. I'm ugly." I kept encouraging Marilyn to try it, and gradually she was able to look at herself for longer periods of time. At first she hated the person she saw in the mirror, because she only saw the reflection of her parents' disapproval toward her. But after allowing herself to feel and express her anger toward her parents and to give them back the projections they had placed on her, Marilyn began to see an entirely different person in the mirror, someone she actually began to like. Eventually, Marilyn was able to gaze into the mirror and say, "I love you"—an exercise I encourage you to practice as well.

EXERCISE: MIRROR, MIRROR

1. Look at yourself in the mirror (you can use a full-length mirror or a smaller one—whichever is the less threatening). If you don't like what you see, try to find at least one thing about yourself you like. Say out loud, "I like my eyes." If you are like Marilyn and can't look at yourself in the mirror without feeling self-hatred or contempt, try to find one thing about yourself you can feel neutral about and say, "I feel neutral about my neck."

2. Do this over the course of several weeks until you have found at least five things about your face or body you can say you like or at least feel neutral about.

3. Look at your reflection and say to yourself, "I like you." Even if you don't mean it yet, say it anyway. Notice how you feel emotionally, what feelings come up in your body when you say this to yourself. If you hear a critical inner voice or a parent's voice saying something negative like "How can you say you like yourself when you're no good?" tell that voice, "Shut up!"

4. Repeat this exercise over the course of several weeks, at least once a week until you can say "I like you" to your reflection and really mean it.

14

If You Had Overly Critical, Shaming, or Perfectionistic Parents

Healing the "I Am Bad," "I Am Unacceptable," and "I Am Not Good Enough" Mirrors

> *I tell you there is such a thing as creative hate.*
>
> —WILLA CATHER, *The Song of the Lark*

IN THIS CHAPTER WE WILL FOCUS on repairing the harm to self-esteem and self-image caused by overly critical, shaming, or perfectionistic parents. This will involve giving yourself permission to express your anger at your abusive parents and to work on ridding yourself of the shame instilled in you.

Children respond differently to shaming. Some become angry and direct that anger outward, sometimes in the form of violence against other people. Others direct their anger inward, often leading to a vicious cycle of self-hatred in which the person becomes isolated and withdrawn in order to avoid the possibility of further rejection. The trauma associated with the pain of an intense shame response can lead to all the phenomena we associate with a post-traumatic stress disorder.

Because the wounds that result from the pain of shaming and rejection are especially difficult to heal, people who have experienced intense forms of this pain are often dominated by a desire to avoid further acts of shaming and rejection. They do this by building defensive walls around themselves that keep out rejection but at the same time keep out intimacy and love. In order to begin to tear down these walls, you will need to heal yourself of your shame.

The first step is to understand exactly what that shame is and how to identify it in yourself. Identifying shame is not as easy as identifying some of our other emotions. When we feel strongly shamed, it is common for us to want to hide from others. In fact, the word *shame* is thought to have derived from an Indo-European word meaning "to hide." Here is how one of my clients described the feeling of being shamed: "I just wanted to dig a hole and hide in it." Another client described feeling shamed like this: " I just wish I could disappear. I'm so ashamed I can't look anyone in the eye."

Checking in with your body can help you discover your shame. We tend to feel shame in our bodies as a *sense of dread*, an overwhelming desire to hide or cover our faces, or a pain in the pit of our stomachs. Some people blush, while others experience feelings of nervousness or a choking or suffocating sensation. Others experience what is called a *shame attack*, in which they feel completely overwhelmed with this sense of dread. Commonly reported by people having a shame attack include feelings of being dizzy or spacey, disoriented, and nauseated.

Differentiate between Shame and Guilt

Shame is often confused with guilt, but it is not the same emotion. When we feel guilt, we feel badly about something we did or neglected to do. When we feel shame, we feel badly about who we are. When we feel guilty, we need to learn that it is okay to make mistakes. When we feel shame, we need to learn that it is okay to be who we are.

Another distinction between guilt and shame is that shame comes from public exposure to one's own vulnerability, while guilt is private. It comes from a sense of failing to measure up to our own internal standards. When others "discover" or "know" that you were once helpless, you tend to feel ashamed. You also feel exposed. If, on the other hand, you feel you caused your own problems, you cease to feel as helpless or exposed. After all, you may reason, you brought your pain on yourself.

EXERCISE: How Shame Has Affected You

1. Think about how you have coped with the shame you endured in childhood. How did you defend against the shame?

2. If you internalized the shame, think about the ways shame has affected your self-esteem.

3. If you have externalized the shame, think about the ways you have projected your shame onto others.

4. Notice what triggers shame in you today. Is it criticism from others, being called on your "stuff" (or as one client described it, "Having my covers pulled"), or is it being rejected?

5. When are you most likely to feel shamed? Is it when you are feeling the most insecure? Is it when you are trying to impress someone?

6. Who is most likely to trigger shame in you? Is it the people you care about the most? Or is it the ones you are trying to impress? How about the people you feel inadequate around or who have rejected you in the past?

If You Externalized Your Shame

Some people defend against shame by projecting it on others and by raging at them. If you tend to do this, particularly if you lash out at people or have sudden, unexpected fits of rage, pay attention to the ways in which you convert shame into anger. Do you put down other people because you feel rejected by them? Do you go on a verbal rampage in an attempt to shame anyone who dares to criticize you? Do you yell at anyone who makes you feel inadequate? Do you become difficult or insulting when you feel like a failure? Although it is painful to own up to such behavior, facing the truth will be the first step toward healing.

In order to break the shame/rage cycle, you will need to ask yourself, "What am I ashamed of?" each and every time you get angry. Think of your anger as a red flag, signaling the fact that you are feeling shame. This is especially true whenever you experience sudden bursts of anger or when you become enraged. It may be difficult to find your shame at first, and you may not be feeling shame each time you feel angry, but with some practice you will be able to recognize those times when you are feeling ashamed and discover what has triggered it. Once you've identified the shame/rage connection, you will need to break it. This means you have to stop yourself from becoming angry as a way of defending against your shame. Refer back to the information in chapter 5 on how to feel your shame, and then let it flow out of you. Later on in this chapter I provide suggestions for alleviating your shame.

If You Internalized Your Shame
FROM SELF-BLAME TO ANGER

Self-blame and shame are closely related. Children tend to blame themselves for their parents' behavior, no matter how inappropriate or abusive. Self-blame is also consistent with the way traumatized people of all ages tend to think. They search for faults in their own behavior in an effort to make sense out of what happened to them. When a child is chronically abused, neither time nor experience provide any corrective for this tendency toward self-blame; instead, it is continually reinforced. The abused child's sense of inner badness may be directly confirmed by parental scapegoating. Survivors frequently describe being blamed not only for their parents' abusiveness or violence but also for other family misfortunes.

Sometimes a child growing up in a blaming family will learn to blame herself—to internalize rather than externalize blame—as a way of avoiding blame from significant others. Such a person learns that if she is quick enough to blame herself, a parent's accusations will subside or be altogether avoided. It is as though the child makes an implicit contract with the parent: I will do the blaming so you will not have to. In this way, the intolerable blaming, which induces shame in the child, is placed under the child's own internal control. It becomes internalized in such a way that the child's inner life is forever subjected to spontaneous self-blame.

If you have a tendency toward self-blame, turning your shame to anger can be a positive and powerful way to rid yourself of shame. Instead of taking the negative energy in, against yourself, the energy is directed outward, toward the person who is doing the shaming or causing the shame.

How to Rid Yourself of Shame

The following suggestions will help you begin working on alleviating or reducing your shame.

1. *Accept the fact that you did not deserve the abuse or neglect.* Tell yourself that nothing you did as a child warranted any kind of abuse or neglect that you experienced. If you continue to blame yourself for your parents' inappropriate or inadequate behavior, you may need to get in touch with how vulnerable and innocent children are. Spend some time around children who were the age you were when you were neglected or emotionally abused. Notice how vulnerable and innocent children really are, no matter how mature they try to act.

2. *Tell significant others about the abuse and neglect you experienced.* As the saying goes, "We are only as sick as our secrets." By keeping hidden from your close friends and family the fact that you were emotionally abused or neglected as a child, you perpetuate the idea that you are keeping it secret because *you* did something wrong. By sharing your experience with someone you love and trust (your partner, a close friend, a therapist,

members of a support group), you will get rid of the secret and get rid of your shame.

3. *Give back your parent's shame.* When a parent abuses a child, it is often because he or she is in the middle of a shame attack. In essence, the parent is projecting his or her shame onto the child. While the abuse is taking place, the child often feels the shame of the abuser and is overwhelmed by it—causing the child to actually take on the shame of the abuser. You may have been told many times by your therapist, or by your friends and loved ones, that the abuse or neglect you endured was not your fault. Now is the time to start believing it. Releasing your anger toward your parents or other abusers will help you stop blaming yourself, because the abuser is the appropriate target for your anger. In getting angry at your abusers, you will affirm your innocence.

4. *Trade self-criticism for compassion and self-acceptance.* In order to heal your shame, it is very important that you trade your tendency to be impatient or self-critical for compassion for yourself. Remember the way you felt when your parents talked to you in an impatient or critical way. Take out pictures of yourself when you were a child and remind yourself that you were an innocent, vulnerable child who did not deserve to be insulted, humiliated, criticized, or shamed for just being who she or he was. Continue to work on replacing the critical or demanding voice inside your head with a more nurturing, compassionate inner voice. Having compassion for yourself will give you the strength and motivation to change, whereas self-criticism will only continue to tear you down.

5. *Stop comparing yourself to others.* People with a great deal of shame react to the awareness of differences between themselves and others by automatically translating it into a comparison of good versus bad, better versus worse. Rather than valuing the differences, they feel threatened by them. But neither you nor the other person needs to emerge as the lesser if your awareness of your differences can remain just that—differences to be owned and valued.

6. *Expect others to accept you as you are.* In order to heal your shame, you also need to consciously work on believing that it is okay to be who you are. This means you need to stop relying on anyone who treats you as if you are not okay the way you are. Surround yourself with people who like and accept you just as you are, as opposed to people who are critical, judgmental, perfectionistic, or otherwise shaming. Open up and deepen your relationships with these people. When someone treats you well, make sure you absorb it. When someone does something nice for you or says something nice about you, take a deep breath and let in the good feelings. When you are alone, remember the positive or kind things the person said or did.

How to Deal with a Shame Attack

If you are having a full-blown shame attack, you may need to talk to a *trusted* friend or someone else close to you (your therapist, your sponsor, a member of your support group, someone at a hotline). Explain that you are having a shame attack and that you are feeling horrible about yourself. Don't blame the person who triggered your shame for making you feel bad (unless it is the same person who shamed you horribly as a child), but take responsibility for your own shame. Try to make a connection between this current incident and what it is reminding you of (from childhood, or from a more recent traumatic shaming). Ask the person to remind you that you are not a horrible person. If it is someone close to you, ask him or her to remind you of your positive attributes.

If you can't find someone you trust to talk to, write down your feelings. Describe what you are feeling in detail, including your physical reactions. Trace these reactions back to other times and incidents when you felt similar feelings. If you find a connecting situation, write about it in detail. Then spend some time reminding yourself of your good qualities and accomplishments.

Countering Messages from Perfectionistic Parents

There is a reason I include ways to overcome the damage caused by perfectionistic parents in this chapter on overcoming the damage caused by overly critical, shaming parents. It is that perfectionism can be extremely shaming. In addition, some people fight against shame by striving for perfection as a way to compensate for an underlying sense of defectiveness. The reasoning goes like this: "If I can become perfect, I am no longer vulnerable to being shamed." Unfortunately, the quest for perfection is doomed to fail, and the realization of this failure reawakens the already present sense of shame the person was trying to run from in the first place. Because he already feels that he is inherently not good enough as a person, nothing he does is ever seen as good enough.

If you expect perfection from yourself, you will be constantly disappointed in yourself and constantly damaging your self-esteem. If you expect perfection from others, you will end up being demanding and critical. If you do this with your children, you will be emotionally abusing them.

How to Deal with Your Internalized Inner Critic

If one or both of your parents was perfectionistic, you will tend to be perfectionistic as well. You'll expect yourself to do things right the first time, and when you make a mistake you will not be forgiving of yourself. Instead, you'll berate yourself with comments like "What's wrong with you?" and "Stupid, you can't do anything right." You may expect perfection from others, but mostly you will expect it from yourself, and your self-chastisement can sometimes be brutal, causing you to become depressed or despondent when you make a mistake. While others seem to be able to move on after making a mistake, you tend to dwell on it, and this continually damages your self-esteem.

If this describes you, the first thing you need to do is identify your inner critic—that harsh, judgmental voice that insists on perfection. Begin to notice how often you berate yourself. Like my client Pamela, you may find it is constant: "I am so hard on myself! Whenever I make a mistake I hear a voice inside my head telling me what an idiot I am—how I can't do anything right—that I am an incompetent fool. I just don't ever let myself off the hook."

Earlier in the book I presented several exercises and processes to help you begin to deal constructively with your internalized inner critic and to begin to form a more positive self-image. This also involves beginning to develop a nurturing inner mother to replace a critical, shaming one, and a safe, powerful internal father to replace one who was judgmental and rigid. Review those portions of the book and continue to provide yourself the nurturing and limits that will help you overcome your shaming experiences.

15

If You Had a Self-Absorbed or Narcissistic Parent

Healing the "I Don't Matter" Mirror

WHEN I WAS GROWING UP I knew my mother hated me. I knew that she wanted to destroy me. I would sometimes catch her looking at me with disdain and malice in her eyes. I suffered from chronic bronchitis and would cough throughout the night and sometimes have fevers. One night my mother came to my bedside to put a cold washcloth on my head to bring down my temperature. In my fevered state I was certain that she was trying to strangle me; I screamed and pushed her away. You could say I was delusional because of my fever, and this was certainly possible. But I also believed my mother would have liked to strangle me.

Many narcissistic parents want to destroy their children. They do not want them to exist. In order to take care of a child, parents frequently must put their own needs aside. Narcissistic parents resent having to do this, because they tend to be selfish and self-absorbed— only their needs count. At the same time, narcissistic parents want their children to be at their beck and call and to take care of *their* needs. While many narcissistic parents resent having to take care of their children, they grow to expect that their children will take care of them.

As a child of a narcissist, your biggest challenge will be to free yourself from the grip of your parent's stranglehold on you. Narcissistic parents do not want their children to have a separate self. They want complete control over their children, to ensure they will be available to satisfy their needs. If a child develops a separate life, she will not be as responsive to her parents' needs.

Creating a Separate Self

In *Trapped in the Mirror*, Elan Golumb compares children of narcissists with bonsai plants: "We are like bonsai plants with prior years of confinements, suppression and reshaping. What is our natural shape? It takes years to uncover as we revert by degrees to growing."

Because most children of narcissists do not really know who they are and because we are so disconnected from our true selves, it is difficult to create a separate self. This is partly due to the judgments our parents placed on us that, in turn, colored our perceptions of ourselves. You most likely learned self-hatred without even knowing who your self really is. You absorbed your parents' negative opinions about you and now believe them to be true. You may have taken on your parents' values but do not really know what you yourself believe in.

Much of the information and exercises in chapter 6 will help you begin to discover who you are separate from your narcissistic parent. In this chapter I will offer you still more suggestions.

Separate Yourself from Your Parents and Your Parents' Opinions of You

Narcissistic parents insist that they know their children better than anyone else. While parents do tend to know their children the best, this is not the case with narcissistic parents, because they project their own self-hatred onto their children and therefore have such distorted perceptions of them.

Unfortunately, children of narcissistic parents, like all children, tend to believe what their parents tell them about themselves. Therefore, one of your most difficult tasks will be to learn to carefully consider the information you received from your parents and to discard the things that are not true. If you remain confused, it will help to get feedback from your closest friends about how they perceive you.

Don't Be Afraid to Look Inside

Children of narcissists are fearful of looking inside, of really getting to know their true selves, often because what they tend to find is a deep anger or rage toward their oppressive parent.

Karen knew that she had a narcissistic mother who despised her and verbally and physically attacked her almost daily. But Karen was afraid to explore the anger she felt toward her mother. She vividly remembered an incident when she experienced an overwhelming desire to murder her mother. She was only six years old, but her mother already had her working in the kitchen, cutting up vegetables. She wasn't doing it to her mother's satisfaction and so her mother was yelling at her, telling her what a stupid child she was, how she could never do anything right. "My hand starting shaking as I listened to her put me down one more time. I put my finger on the sharp tip of the knife and then I imagined taking the knife and stabbing my mother in the heart. The more I thought about it, the more my hand shook. But my legs felt like cement. I couldn't move off the place where I was standing. Thank God, because if I had been able to move I think I would have stabbed her."

It took a lot of encouraging from me for Karen to begin to own and express the rage she still felt toward her mother. She was afraid her rage would burst out of her and cause her to lose control. "I never want to feel that kind of murderous rage again," she would tell me. Eventually, through journaling and anger letters Karen was able to put her feelings down on paper. "I do have a lot of rage and it is murderous," she shared with me, "but now I know my rage is justified and I know how to contain it."

Others are afraid their narcissistic parent will sense their anger and that this might cause a further attack. Stills others disown their anger, because being angry makes them too much like the parent they abhor. This is what my client William told me when I suggested he needed to express his pent-up anger toward his father. "I refuse to be like my father. He was angry all the time and he was constantly hurting people with his comments. That's why I decided I'd just bury my anger and never dig it up."

The truth is, you cannot have been raised by a narcissistic parent without experiencing tremendous rage toward him or her. You must accept that anger is a part of life and part of yourself. Refer back to chapter 5 for suggestions on how you can express your anger in safe and healthy ways and find a way that works for you. It can help to ask your body how it would like to release the anger (hitting, throwing, smashing, tearing). You intuitively know just what you need to do. If you have had a history of losing control of your anger, chose an anger-release technique that does not involve physical activity, such as journaling or anger letters.

Mourn the Loss of a Healthy Childhood

In order to free yourself from your narcissistic parent, you must mourn the possibility that you will ever have a happy childhood with loving, accepting parents. Mourn the loss of the fantasy that your parent will love you today in the ways that you need. Continuing to fantasize about your narcissistic parent one day changing and treating you the way you've always hoped for will keep you stuck in the past and unable to create a separate life from him or her.

Separate Yourself from Your Parents' Values, False Beliefs, and Negative Habits

It is also important for you to stop being invisible to your parents out of your need to please or appease them. Dare to have your own ideas and goals. Your parents won't like this and may increase their attempts to squash you, but remind yourself that you are an adult and that they do not have power over you today.

Narcissistic parents cannot allow their children to be independent beings. After all, what if they do something of which they disapprove? What if it is something they cannot do themselves? Out of their need to bind their children to them, narcissistic parents will convince their children that they cannot make it without their parent, that they are incompetent or inadequate, or that no one will ever want them. Don't continue to believe these things about yourself. Dare to experiment with new people and new ways of thinking. Refer back to chapter 4 for more information on how to do this.

Allow Yourself to Experience Life

Sometimes experience is necessary in order to find out what we are lacking. Experience confronts what we are taught to believe. For example, travel teaches us how people can live in non-narcissistic ways. And being physically far away from your parents can make you feel that you are beyond your parents' reach, so far that you can try out different ways of being.

I am at my best when I travel. I feel excited and open and independent. My personality takes on a subtle but profound change. I'm more friendly than I am at home. I am more open to meeting and talking to strangers. I feel more energy and I take greater risks.

Children of narcissistic parents benefit from stepping into the unknown of any type, be it people, reading, experimenting, or playing musical instruments. My experience with learning how to swim is an excellent example of how stepping out can help us to individuate. I realized that the reason swimming was so powerful for me (and caused my inner saboteur to rear his ugly head) was that it was completely separate from any association with my mother. I never swam with her. It was my own territory, and learning how to swim was nothing my mother would have ever done. Swimming was all mine. It was not polluted by her criticism, expectations, or fears. In the warm, sensuous water I am on my own, unencumbered by my mother's incessant voice. I am connected to my body in a sensuous way, something that was forbidden by my mother. I am free, I am me, and I am in my body. What a wonderful experience!

Explore Your Creativity

The same joy can be true of creating, whether it is music, art, or writing. If you are not connected to your creativity, you can become increasingly dependent on your narcissistic parents to give you what needs to come from within. Creativity is an incredibly effective way of "stepping out and away" from your parents and becoming a separate self. The act of creating is itself an act of individuation.

As Elan Golumb so eloquently stated, "Creativity takes the destructive threads of life and puts them together with something from within that changes it all into what can sustain a faltering self. Our creative mind bypasses hackneyed limited thought and shows us who we really are. . . . To one who thinks herself worthless, seeing her creativity is a shock. Where did this outpouring come from? Is there a worthwhile self?"

Work on discovering what interests you, what creates passion within you. Take back your self. Because it was no doubt difficult for you to take on any project without parental invasion, you may have rejected interests, hobbies, and even talents in an effort to separate from your parents. Now it is time to take back these interests and hobbies.

Join a Group

Whether it is group therapy, a 12-step group, or a spirituality circle, in order to develop a healthier self you need places where you can discover who you really are and are encouraged to express how you really feel. You need feedback from others that supports your developing sense of self. This will include feedback that will correct your distorted, unacceptable self-image. Most important, because adult children of narcissists tend to be self-destructive, isolated, and disconnected from life and from others, you need connection with others. And you desperately need the experience of being recognized and accepted by others.

Focus on Establishing an Inner Life

Most children of narcissists have not established an inner life. You can do this by discovering your feelings, thoughts, and dreams. Instead of allowing the television or Internet to absorb your attention and distract you from yourself, go for a solitary walk. Write in your journal. Read a novel or a self-help book. Learn to meditate. Creating a strong inner life will help you separate from your narcissistic parent and discover your true self.

Seek Outside Help

Your efforts to heal your wounds and to become a separate self from your narcissistic parent may be limited by self-protective and counterproductive defenses of which you may be unaware. A professional psychotherapist can help you identify these defenses and work past them.

Unfortunately, if you had a narcissistic parent is it likely that you will have some strong narcissistic tendencies yourself. Because of this, your inner world may be quite empty. Your true self may be dysfunctional, and you may have created a tyrannical and delusional false self in its stead. You may find it difficult to love others, because you can't love yourself. Instead you love your reflection, your surrogate self. Mirror work can help you to confront this false self and to replace it with a real self:

- Look in the mirror and ask yourself, "Who am I?"
- Look deep into your eyes to find the real person there.

It can be uncomfortable or even painful to look into your eyes so deeply and face what you see there. You may see pain, fear, or rage. I will never forget the first time I looked deep in my mirror. I awoke in the middle of the night and needed to go to the bathroom. Afterward I felt compelled to look deep into my eyes. I was horrified with what I saw. I barely recognized myself. Instead I saw someone who was filled with rage and malice. Fortunately, I was working with a Jungian psychologist at the time and had begun to own my dark side or shadow, so I knew that what I was looking at was all my repressed rage at my mother.

You may not like what or who you see at first. Like me, you may become overwhelmed by the rage you find hiding in your eyes. But once you find that rage, you can begin to release it in constructive ways. Once the rage has subsided you can look even deeper to find your true self and your true essence.

You may also find that you have difficulty living in the present. Instead, life is a constant struggle, a striving, a drive for something. You may tend to take your behavioral, emotional, and cognitive cues exclusively from others.

As can be expected, we learned many of our narcissistic parents' habits. We develop narcissistic defenses and patterns of perception that make us behave insensitively toward others. Like prisoners of war, we take on the stance of our captors in order to deny our vulnerability. We identify with our aggressors. We acquired the parental traits that caused us most pain.

Relationships with others will likely be very difficult for you. You may find that you feel smothered in intimate relationships and at the same time have a tremendous fear of abandonment. Children of narcissists can be as critical and perfectionistic as their parents. You may be intolerant of the mistakes of others and may have a cynical outlook on life, and this may make it difficult for you to get along with others. At the same time, you may be hypersensitive to comments others make and may assume that others are against you, even when they are not. Your years of being corrected or ignored by your narcissistic parents may cause you to believe that others are treating you in the same way.

A professional psychotherapist who has been trained to work with children of narcissistic parents and with people who have narcissistic tendencies can help you overcome your similarities to your parent and create a self that is sensitive to the feelings of others. If you have acquired some narcissistic tendencies, treatment will be difficult because it will require you to admit your human failings and to recognize your need for other people. It will also mean once more experiencing the feelings of being a helpless and manipulated child. This can be extremely painful, but the rewards are certainly worth it. You will also need to recognize the emptiness of life compulsively controlled by the need for admiration and achievement. As Golumb wrote, "The outcome of her struggle to uncover an authentic self will be the ability to lead an ordinary life, one with real joys and sorrows, not the fictitious pleasures of a mirrored image."

I am pleased to tell you that with the help of both individual and group therapy, creativity, journaling, traveling, meeting in support circles, the Solutions Program, and my conscious efforts to find my true self, I have made great headway in separating myself from my narcissistic mother. I have worked long and hard on my own tendency to be critical and perfectionistic and I no longer define my life by my accomplishments. By following the suggestions outlined here and with the aid of a good therapist, I am convinced that the same can be true for you.

Healing my narcissistic wounds has been the most difficult aspect of my personal recovery—even more difficult than healing from the childhood sexual abuse I experienced. While writing this book I dreamed about my struggle. I was being confronted by three friends from my past with the fact that I, too, had problems (I think this was in reference to the fact that I continue to see clients). I admitted to them that, yes, I did have a problem—that I had difficulty trusting anyone. I confronted each friend with evidence as to why I shouldn't trust anyone by citing how each friend had betrayed me. The next scene in the dream involved the three people looking down at me. I had had all my skin removed and I was lying on a bed literally stripped bare. I believe this was symbolic of showing that I was willing to create a new start in life—that I was willing to let go of my belief that I could not trust anyone. A banquet hall was set up and I was led in with soft towels on my back. There were three separate tables set up. I was going to sit down with each of the three people separately and mend our relationship.

My difficulty trusting others was just one of the many problems I've experienced due to being raised by a narcissistic mother. But with continued work on myself I am experiencing healing with every passing day. I am convinced that you can, too.

16

Continuing to Heal

As you have discovered from reading this book, you do not have to remain trapped by reflections from the past. You have the power to raise your self-esteem, improve your self-image, quiet the nagging critic within, and heal your shame. Low self-esteem is not proof of your value but rather a reflection of the way you were treated as a child and the judgments and unreasonable expectations placed on you.

You cannot afford to ignore the negative attitudes and beliefs you have toward yourself. These attitudes and beliefs were learned, and they can be unlearned. By remembering to bring up a nurturing inner voice to comfort and encourage yourself, you can continue to counter the negative inner critic. By using a self-cherishing tone with yourself, you can provide the nourishment and power you need to change.

In order to continue to feel better about yourself, surround yourself with people who like you and treat you with respect. Allow yourself to experience and take in the feeling of being enjoyed. Get involved in activities that provide you with a feeling of competence and achievement.

Although being around others who accept and enjoy you and having experiences with success will be important in your personal growth, it is crucial that you do not allow others' mirrors to totally influence your image of yourself. Remember, every person will see you to some extent through his or her own personal filters and needs.

It is vital that you remember that any one person's view of you is only *one* of the many reflections coming your way. Because the mirrors of other people may contain some distortions, as did your parents' mirrors, these other views of you may not always be accurate.

It is also important that you continue to learn to love and value yourself just because you exist. This appreciation comes when you view yourself as special and precious—even though you may not approve of everything you do. It requires sensing your uniqueness and finding it dear. In spite of your flaws and foibles, remain open to the wonder of you.

Start by asking yourself, "How much do I value myself?" Appreciate the fact that there is no other person on earth who is quite like you.

Writing Exercise: Your Special Qualities

1. To help you more in this healing, make a list of your special qualities as a person—those things that make you distinctly you. No matter how difficult it may still be to make this list, the truth is you do have certain capacities and sensitivities that are uniquely yours. You do have special strengths that in some way differ from the strengths of others.

2. If you have trouble writing this list, ask a close friend to see if you can work together to make a list of your special qualities.

3. Place your list of positive attributes and special qualities on your bathroom or bedroom mirror so that you can remind yourself every day of what a wonderful person you really are. Read the list out loud on those days when you are most critical of yourself or when you doubt your specialness.

If you are like most people, you have spent years focusing on the qualities you don't possess. Now, reverse your focus and concentrate on the positive qualities you do possess. Stop taking yourself for granted and begin to acknowledge all the hard work you have done to get this far. Give yourself credit for surviving your childhood, for continuing to work on yourself, for reading this book.

Remember to treat yourself with respect. Quietly, yet firmly, ask others to show respect for your needs. Continue to catch yourself in the act when you begin to criticize yourself. Continue to respect your body's physical and emotional needs and actively work on meeting them. Carve out blocks of time for doing things that make you feel good about yourself and spend time with others who enjoy you. Reward yourself from time to time for doing a good job of taking care of yourself.

I hope that by reading this book and completing the exercises and assignments you have already begun to notice some small differences in how you feel about yourself. On the other hand, change does take time, especially when you are making significant changes to your self-esteem, attempting to quiet your inner critic and heal your shame. Be patient with yourself as you continue to work on this process. Don't add to your shame or give voice to your inner critic by chastising yourself for not getting better sooner. We rarely feel as if we are gaining headway when we are in the middle of recovery. It is usually only when we look back on our lives that we can see the consistent growth.

I also suggest you reread the chapters that apply to you the most or that you had the most difficulties with. If you have not completed the exercises, I encourage you to do so. The exercises not only help you understand yourself better, they also give direction for further work on yourself.

If you find that your self-concept has become inflexible and you cannot accept positive evidence about your worth and value, I encourage you to seek professional help. I list a few avenues for such help in the appendix.

I welcome your feedback. Please e-mail me at beverly@ beverlyengel.com. Check out my Web site, www.beverlyengel.com, for listings of workshops, announcements, and my mailing address.

Finally, I wish to share with you this poem:

OPEN HEARTS
by Therese Blackwell Mietus

Come close beloved children
To the Heart of the Mother within

Breathe in the Golden Sunrise
To cleanse this world of "sin"

For deep within the Heart of you
There is no sin of course

Just pure and eternal Essence
Connected to the Source

It has to do with an innocence
The pure, open Heart of a child

Compassionate words, empathetic deeds
A World of trust so mild

So come with me and remember
That World of what's to be

Can't you feel within your Heart
The Child Heart of me?

Now, breathe out the Golden Sunset
And our darkness of the past

So we can go back Home again
Together, forever, at last!

You are the Essence of all that has ever been

Appendix

Recommended Therapies

You can't expect to achieve complete recovery from one self-help book. If you find that you need help in any area, do not hesitate to seek professional help. I recommend the following types of therapy.

Mirror Therapy

In this book I have given you the basic concepts of Mirror Therapy as it applies to raising your self-esteem, improving your self-image (including your body image), quieting your inner critic, and healing your shame. But Mirror Therapy was developed to help survivors of emotional abuse to heal all aspects of their lives, including their relationships with others. In the near future I plan on writing another book that will focus more on these and other aspects of Mirror Therapy. For example, in order to maintain healthy relationships we need to add the following truths to our model:

- Human beings are incredibly resilient. Given empathy and appropriate guidance, people with emotionally impoverished childhoods can learn how to express their emotions, develop compassion for self and others, and expand their empathy.

- Because the emotionally abused or neglected often do not learn how to take care of themselves, they find it difficult to care for others when they are hurt or distressed. Instead, their focus remains riveted on their own unmet needs and desires.

- Sometimes, in order to be able to have empathy and compassion for others, we must first learn to give these things to ourselves. As adults, we often find that others treat us in ways that reflect the way we feel about ourselves. Therefore, if we want others to treat us with respect and kindness, we must first start giving these things to ourselves.

If you would like more information on Mirror Therapy contact me at:

P.O. Box 6412, Los Osos, CA 93412-6412,
beverly@beverlyengel.com.

Voice Therapy

The clinical psychologist Robert Firestone's pioneer work in identifying the origins and destructiveness of the inner critic led to his process "voice therapy." In voice therapy, clients are taught to externalize their inner critical thoughts. By doing so they expose their self-attacks and ultimately develop ways to change their negative attitude about themselves into a more objective, nonjudgmental view. As the voice of the inner critic is externalized through verbalization, intense feelings are released that can result in powerful emotional catharsis, accompanied by important insights. (Firestone's methods are primarily used in the context of individual and group therapy. I include here some adaptations of his methods that you can try on your own.)

Voice therapy is a method of eliciting and assessing pervasive negative thought processes that represent an alien part of the personality (an inner saboteur). The method combines cognitive, affective, and behavioral components into an integrated treatment strategy. Voice therapy includes the following steps:

1. Identify the negative thought patterns that regulate maladaptive, self-destructive behavior, and encourage the release of the negative affect associated with this thinking process.

2. Trace these destructive thoughts to their origin; that is, patients identify the source of these thoughts and attitudes in their early experiences. They discuss their personal insights and identify the self-defeating or self-destructive patterns that the negative thoughts predispose.

3. The final step makes up the majority of therapeutic work. Attempt to implement behavioral change in a direction that

counters these destructive thought processes and leads to a more constructive ways of fulfilling one's goals and potentialities.

The techniques of voice therapy bring internalized, negative thought processes to the surface with accompanying affect in a dialogue format so the patient can confront elements of the personality that are antagonistic toward the self. It is referred to as voice therapy because it is a process of giving language or spoken words to critical thought patterns that are at the core of an individual's defensive behavior and lifestyle. This method can be used in a variety of clinical populations and is particularly valuable in understanding and working with patients with depression and diverse forms of substance abuse.

Firestone is the author of six books and over twenty published articles, and the producer at the Glendon Association of thirty-five video documentaries used for training mental health professionals. To learn more about voice therapy, you can read his book *Voice Therapy: A Psychological Approach to Self-Destructive Behavior*, or you can contact him at the Glendon Association through their Web site, www .glendon.org.

The Solutions Program

The Solutions Program can help if you would like more assistance learning how to self-nurture and set more effective limits (especially important for those with an eating disorder). If we have not mastered two skills—*self-nurturing* and *effective limit setting*—we cannot soothe and comfort ourselves from within. Consequently, it is only natural that that we will tend to soothe and comfort ourselves by overeating, drinking, spending, overworking, and smoking, or by people-pleasing, rescuing others, putting up walls, or thinking too much.

The Solutions Program was developed over the last twenty years at one of the nation's most prestigious medical schools, the University of California, San Francisco, School of Medicine. Emerging understandings of neurobiology suggest that using the skills over the long term may retrain the elusive *feeling brain* to spontaneously favor a life of emotional balance, relationship intimacy, spiritual connection, and freedom from excessive appetites.

By using the self-nurturing and effective limit-setting skills, over time they become automatic. When they do, we spontaneously soothe and comfort ourselves *internally* so we no longer need the common *external* solutions to distress.

I recommend that you read the book *The Pathway: Follow the Road to Health and Happiness* by Laurel Mellin, M.A., R.D., to learn about what she calls "cycles" (the nurturing cycle and the limits cycle). If you want more support, there are hundreds of Solutions groups nationwide led by health professionals, as well as self-help Solutions Circles and an active Internet community.

For more information, read *The Pathway: Follow the Road to Health and Happiness* or contact the Institute for Health Solutions at (415) 457-3331, www.thepathway.org

Treatment of Post-traumatic Stress Disorder

Emotional abuse can cause a person to suffer from post-traumatic stress disorder. In addition, many who were emotionally abused as children were physically or sexually abused as well. There are several treatment options.

Cognitive Behavioral Therapy (CBT)

Increasingly used in the treatment of dissociative disorders (DID) and borderline personality disorder (BPD), dysfunctional and mal-adaptive behaviors, thoughts, and beliefs are replaced by more adaptive ones. *Exposure therapy* is one form of CBT unique to trauma treatment that uses careful, repeated, detailed imagining of the trauma (exposure) in a safe, controlled context, to help the survivor face and gain control of the fear and distress that was overwhelming in the trauma. Along with exposure, CBT for trauma includes learning skills for coping with anxiety (such as breathing retraining or biofeedback) and negative thoughts (cognitive restructuring), managing anger, preparing for stress reactions (stress inoculation), and handling future trauma symptoms, as well as addressing urges to use alcohol or drugs when they occur (relapse prevention), and communicating and relating effectively with people (social skills and marital therapy).

Eye Movement Desensitization and Reprocessing (EMDR)

This is an interactional method that accelerates the treatment of a wide range of pathologies and self-esteem issues related to past events and present conditions. Numerous studies show that it is effective in the rapid desensitization of traumatic events, including a cognitive restructuring and a reduction of client symptoms.

The procedure produces rapid eye movements in a client while a traumatic memory is recalled and processed. This technique seems to lessen the amount of therapeutic time needed to process and resolve traumatic memories. Developed by Francine Shapiro, this technique requires training and following of specific protocols for appropriate use. For more information, contact:

EMDR Centers

P.O. Box 141743

Austin, TX 78714-1743

(512) 451-6944 (to obtain a referral in your area).

Treatment for Borderline Personality Disorder: Dialectic Behavioral Therapy (DBT)

Although the term *borderline personality disorder* is sometimes considered pejorative, there is no question that people (mostly women) who carry this label are highly distressed and in a great deal of emotional and even physical pain. Regardless of what you believe about the label of borderline, the skills developed by Marsha Linehan to treat this disorder are highly effective. The people who commit to doing the skills training offered in dialectic behavioral therapy (DBT) groups get better. Most mental health centers now offer these groups. Refer to Linehan's *Skills Training Manual for Treating Borderline Personality Disorder* (New York: Guilford Press, 1993) for more information on this form of therapy.

References

1 OUR PARENTS AS MIRRORS

Loring, Marti Tamm, *Emotional Abuse: The Trauma and the Treatment* (San Francisco: Jossey-Bass, 1998).

Napier, Nancy, *Recreating Your Self: Help for Adult Children of Dysfunctional Families* (New York: W.W. Norton and Co., 1990).

Wisechild, Louise, *The Mother I Carry: A Memoir of Healing from Emotional Abuse* (Seattle, Wash.: Seal Press, 1993).

2 THE SEVEN TYPES OF NEGATIVE PARENTAL MIRRORS

Golumb, Elan, Ph.D., *Trapped in the Mirror: Adult Children of Narcissists in Their Struggle for Self* (New York: William Morrow, 1992).

Kaufman, Gershen, *Shame: The Power of Caring* (Cambridge, Mass.: Schenkman Publishing Co., 1980).

4 HOW MIRROR THERAPY WORKS

Middleton-Moz, Jane, *Shame and Guilt: Masters of Disguise* (Deerfield Beach, Fla.: Health Communications, Inc., 1990).

5 REJECTING YOUR PARENTS' NEGATIVE REFLECTION

Brown, Byron, *Soul Without Shame: A Guide to Liberating Yourself from the Judge Within* (Boston: Shambhala, 1999).

6 EMOTIONALLY SEPARATING FROM YOUR PARENTS

Brown, Byron, *Soul without Shame*.

Engel, Beverly, *Breaking the Cycle of Abuse* (Hoboken, N.J.: John Wiley & Sons, 2005).

Goleman, Daniel, *Emotional Intelligence: Why It Can Matter More than IQ* (New York: Bantam Books, 1995).

7 QUIETING AND COUNTERING YOUR INNER CRITIC

Golumb, *Trapped in the Mirror*.

Mellin, Laurel, *The Pathway: Follow the Road to Health and Happiness* (New York: Regan Books, 2003).

13 IF YOU WERE OVERLY CONTROLLED OR TYRANNIZED: HEALING THE "I AM POWERLESS" MIRROR

Love, Patricia, *The Emotional Incest Syndrome: What to Do When a Parent's Love Rules Your Life* (New York: Bantam Books, 1990).

Golumb, *Trapped in the Mirror*.

Recommended Reading

RECOVERY FROM CHILDHOOD ABUSE

Farmer, Steven. *Adult Children of Abusive Parents: A Healing Program for Those Who Have Been Physically, Sexually or Emotionally Abused*. Los Angeles: Lowell House, 1989.

Forward, Susan. *Toxic Parents: Overcoming Their Hurtful Legacy and Reclaiming Your Life*. New York: Bantam, 1989.

Miller, Alice. *The Drama of the Gifted Child*, rev. ed. New York: Basic Books, 1994.

———. *For Your Own Good*, 3rd. ed. New York: Noonday Press, 1990.

Napier, Nancy, *Recreating Your Self: Help for Adult Children of Dysfunctional Families*. New York: W.W. Norton and Co., 1990.

CONTROLLING PARENTS

Neuharth, Dan. *If You Had Controlling Parents: How to Make Peace with Your Past and Take Your Place in the World*. New York: HarperCollins, 1998.

NARCISSISM

Brown, Nina. *Children of the Self-Absorbed: A Grownup's Guide to Getting Over Narcissistic Parents*. Oakland, Calif.: New Harbinger, 2001.

Golumb, Elan. *Trapped in the Mirror: Adult Children of Narcissists in Their Struggle for Self*. New York: William Morrow, 1992.

EMOTIONAL INCEST

Love, Patricia. *The Emotional Incest Syndrome: What to Do When a Parent's Love Rules Your Life*. New York: Bantam, 1990.

MEMOIRS ON HEALING FROM EMOTIONAL ABUSE

Wisechild, Louise. *The Mother I Carry: A Memoir of Healing from Emotional Abuse*. Seattle, Wash.: Seal Press, 1993.

SELF-ESTEEM

McKay, Matthew, and Patrick Fanning. *Self-Esteem: A Proven Program of Cognitive Techniques for Assessing, Improving, and Maintaining Self-Esteem*. Oakland, Calif.: New Harbinger, 2000.

BODY IMAGE

McFarland, Barbara, and Tyeis Baker-Baumann. *Shame and Body Image: Culture and the Compulsive Eater*. Deerfield Beach, Fla.: Health Communications, 1990.

SELF-HELP FOR EMOTIONAL DEFICITS CAUSED BY EMOTIONAL ABUSE AND/OR NEGLECT

Ciaramicoli, Arthur, and Katherine Ketchum. *The Power of Empathy: A Practical Guide to Creating Intimacy, Self-Understanding and Lasting Love*. New York: Dutton, 2000.

Goleman, Daniel. *Emotional Intelligence: Why It Can Matter More Than IQ* New York: Bantam, 1995.

Loring, Marti Tamm. *Emotional Abuse: The Trauma and the Treatment*. San Francisco: Jossey-Bass, 1998.

Mellin, Laurel. *The Pathway: Follow the Road to Health and Happiness*. New York: Regan Books, 2003.

EMOTIONAL ABUSE IN ADULT RELATIONSHIPS

Engel, Beverly. *The Emotionally Abused Woman*. New York: Ballantine, 1990.
———, *The Emotionally Abusive Relationship*. New York: John Wiley & Sons, 2002.

SHAME

Bradshaw, John. *Healing the Shame That Binds You*. Deerfield Beach, Fla.: Health Communications, Inc., 1988.

Brown, Byron. *Soul without Shame: A Guide to Liberating Yourself From the Judge Within*. Boston: Shambhala, 1999.

Kaufman, Gershen. *Shame: The Power of Caring*, Cambridge, Mass.: Schenkman Publishing Co., 1980.

Lewis, Michael. *Shame: The Exposed Self*. New York: Free Press, 1995.

Middleton-Moz, Jane. *Shame and Guilt*. Deerfield Beach, Fla.: Health Communications, Inc., 1990.

Smedes, Lewis B. *Shame and Grace: Healing the Shame We Don't Deserve*. San Francisco: HarperSanFrancisco, 1993.

ANGER

Engel, Beverly. *Honor Your Anger: How Transforming Your Anger Style Can Change Your Life*. Hoboken, N.J.: John Wiley & Sons, 2003.

Harbin, Thomas J. *Beyond Anger: A Guide for Men*. New York: Marlowe and Company, 2000.

Lerner, Harriet Goldhor. *The Dance of Anger: A Woman's Guide to Changing the Patterns of Intimate Relationships*. New York: Harper and Row, 1985.

Williams, Redford, and Virginia Williams. *Anger Kills: 17 Strategies for Controlling the Hostility That Can Harm Your Health*. New York: Harper Paperbacks, 1993.

FORGIVENESS

Klein, Charles. *How to Forgive When You Can't Forget: Healing Our Personal Relationships.* New York: Berkley Publishing Group, 1997.

Safer, Jeanne. *Forgiving and Not Forgiving: A New Approach to Resolving Intimate Betrayal.* New York: Avon, 1999.

Smedes, Lewis B. *Forgive and Forget: Healing the Hurts We Don't Deserve.* San Francisco: Harper and Row, 1984.

RECONCILIATION

Davis, Laura. *I Thought We'd Never Speak Again.* New York: HarperCollins, 2002.

DEALING WITH YOUR ABUSIVE PARENTS TODAY

Bloomfield, Harold. *Making Peace with Your Parents.* New York: Ballantine Books, 1983.

Engel, Beverly. *Divorcing a Parent.* New York: Ballantine Books, 1991.

Secunda, Victoria. *When You and Your Mother Can't Be Friends.* New York: Dell Publishing, 1990.

Index